SANDMAN
MYSTERY
THEATRE

DR. DEATH
-AND-
THE NIGHT
OF THE
BUTCHER

SANDMAN MYSTERY THEATRE:
DR. DEATH AND THE NIGHT OF THE BUTCHER

Front and back cover photos by Gavin Wilson.
Original series covers by Gavin Wilson and Richard Bruning.

Published by DC Comics. Cover and compilation
copyright © 2007 DC Comics. All Rights Reserved.

Originally published in single magazine form as
SANDMAN MYSTERY THEATRE 21-28. Copyright
© 1994, 1995 DC Comics. All Rights Reserved.
All characters, their distinctive likenesses and related
elements featured in this publication are trademarks of
DC Comics. The stories, characters and incidents featured
in this publication are entirely fictional. DC Comics does
not read or accept unsolicited submissions of ideas,
stories or artwork.

DC Comics, 1700 Broadway, New York, NY 10019

A Warner Bros. Entertainment Company

Printed in Canada. First Printing.

ISBN:1-4012-1237-9   ISBN 13: 978-1-4012-1237-7

MATT WAGNER
STEVEN T. SEAGLE
WRITERS

GUY DAVIS
VINCE LOCKE
ARTISTS

DAVID HORNUNG
COLORIST

JOHN COSTANZA
GASPAR SALADINO
LETTERERS

SANDMAN MYSTERY THEATRE

DR. DEATH
—AND—
THE NIGHT OF THE BUTCHER

-DR. DEATH-

WRITTEN BY MATT WAGNER
AND STEVEN T. SEAGLE

LAYOUTS BY GUY DAVIS

ART BY VINCE LOCKE

LETTERING BY GASPAR SALADINO

"Just when you're certain

that your life is as bad

as it can be,

you're shown a glimpse

of how much worse

things *could* go."

There are, of course, two ways to look at this.

On one hand, Wesley is trying to protect me from harm--

--After all, the Sandman does get involved in some awfully frightful endeavors.

On the other hand, Wesley is intentionally lying to me.

Which would mean that despite what he says or does--

--He actually cares little about me.

Of course this isn't exactly the sort of thing one can just bring up over drinks at Rooker's.

"Yes, Wesley... I agree. Busby Berkeley is a genius. Oh, and by the way... you are the Sandman, aren't you?"

Even so, this can't hang like a specter between us. I'm going to have to do something.

DIAN? THAT IS YOU, ISN'T IT?

LUCY? HELLO.

5

MY GOODNESS BUT YOU'RE LOOKING WELL. HOW IS UNCLE BILL?

OH, FATHER'S WELL, THOUGH I'M *SURE* HE WISHES HIS FAVORITE NIECE WOULD DROP BY MORE OFTEN.

YOU'RE RIGHT, I *SHOULD* MAKE TIME FOR A VISIT, BUT I'VE JUST BEEN *FRANTIC.* ARE YOU STILL IN THE COUNTRY?

'WELL...MY *BELONGINGS* ARE STILL ON THE FARM, BUT I'VE BEEN SPENDING MOST OF MY TIME IN THE CITY THESE DAYS.

I'M...*SEEING* SOMEONE SPECIAL, AND I JUST CAN'T STAY AWAY FOR MORE THAN A DAY OR TWO.

THIS MYSTERY MAN SOUNDS LIKE HE'S GOT MY COUSIN'S HEART WRAPPED ROUND HIS INDEX FINGER.

UGH! I FEEL ABSOLUTELY *ANCIENT.*

I COULD HAVE *SWORN* THAT THE LAST TIME I SAW YOU WE WERE STILL PLAYING WITH DOLLS AND TIN HORSES.

I *STILL* LIKE HORSES. ONLY NOW INSTEAD OF TIN, I HAVE A *REAL* ONE. FATHER'S BEEN BREEDING THEM LATELY AS SHOW HORSES.

REALLY? THAT SOUNDS FASCINATING.

OH, IT IS. YOU REALLY SHOULD COME OUT TO THE RANCH SOMETIME AND WE'LL TAKE AN AFTERNOON RIDE. THEY'RE GREAT FOR CLEARING THE HEAD.

YOU KNOW...THAT SOUNDS LIKE THE *EXACT* TREATMENT I NEED FOR MY CURRENT STATE OF MIND. MAYBE I *WILL* COME OUT.

LISTEN, I *HAVE* TO RUN, BUT I'LL PHONE YOU SOON.

OKAY, AND DO COME VISIT. WE NEED TO CATCH UP MORE *FULLY.* I'VE MISSED TALKING TO YOU, DIAN.

SAME HERE, LUCY. YOU TAKE CARE AND I'LL BE IN TOUCH.

Isn't that how it's supposed to be?

2

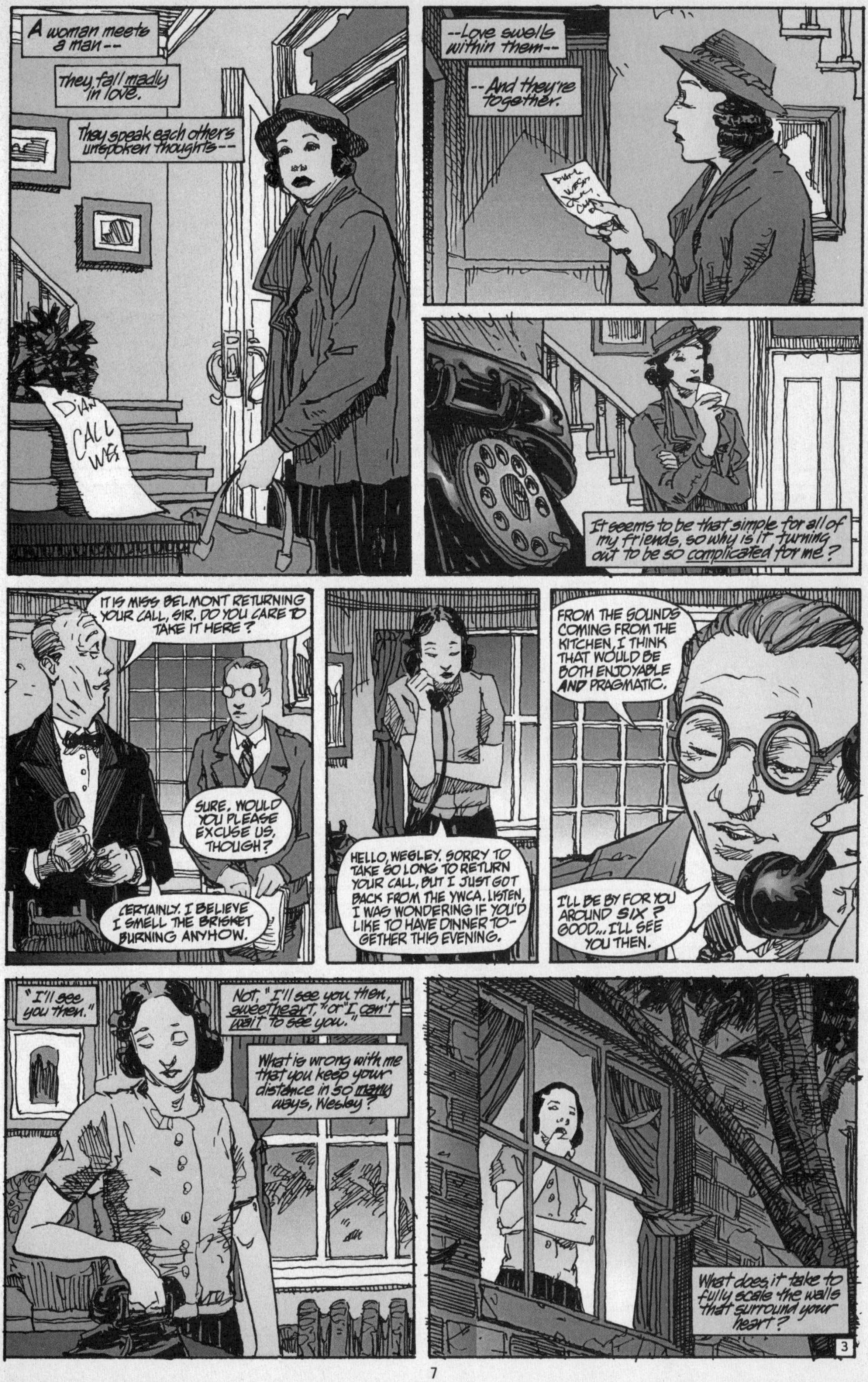
A woman meets a man--
They fall madly in love.
They speak each other's unspoken thoughts--
DIAN CALL WES
--Love swells within them--
--And they're together.
It seems to be that simple for all of my friends, so why is it turning out to be so complicated for me?
IT IS MISS BELMONT RETURNING YOUR CALL, SIR. DO YOU CARE TO TAKE IT HERE?
SURE. WOULD YOU PLEASE EXCUSE US, THOUGH?
CERTAINLY. I BELIEVE I SMELL THE BRISKET BURNING ANYHOW.
HELLO, WESLEY. SORRY TO TAKE SO LONG TO RETURN YOUR CALL, BUT I JUST GOT BACK FROM THE YWCA. LISTEN, I WAS WONDERING IF YOU'D LIKE TO HAVE DINNER TOGETHER THIS EVENING.
FROM THE SOUNDS COMING FROM THE KITCHEN, I THINK THAT WOULD BE BOTH ENJOYABLE AND PRAGMATIC.
I'LL BE BY FOR YOU AROUND SIX? GOOD... I'LL SEE YOU THEN.
"I'll see you then."
Not, "I'll see you then, sweetheart," or "I can't wait to see you."
What is wrong with me that you keep your distance in so many ways, Wesley?
What does it take to fully scale the walls that surround your heart?
3

DR. DEATH
act one

SORRY T' INTERRUPT YOUR READIN'. GOT A PACKAGE FOR SUITE 34.

...JUST A MINNIT... JUST...GOTTA...FINISH PARAGRAPH--

--OKAY. *DELIVERY* YOU SAY? YOU CAN JUST LEAVE IT HERE AN' I'LL TAKE IT UP IN A FEW.

CAN'T *DO* THAT. THIS'S GOTTA BE DELIVERED IN PERSON. MEDICAL SUPPLIES. YOU KNOW.

WELL THEN... GO AHEAD, I GUESS. JUST DON'T TOUCH NOTHIN' UP THERE, HUH?

SURE.

HEY!

SERVICE STAIRS'RE AROUND BACK, BUCK.

SURE. NO PROBLEM. SORRY.

4

--I'LL BE DAMNED...!

PHEW! WISH THEY HAD SOME WATER COOLERS 'ROUND HERE.

...JESUS, WHAT A CLIMB...

DELIVERY!

DR.

TAP TAP TAP

COME IN...

GOT A SPECIAL DELIVERY FOR YOU, DOCTOR. HAD T' BRING IT UP PERSONAL. GUESS YOU KNOW WHY.

I UNDERSTAND. PLEASE, COME IN.

5

YOU LOOK TIRED. ARE YOU FEELING WELL?

IT'S THE CLIMB, DOC. HAD T' TAKE THE SERVICE STAIRS. 'S LEFT ME WINDED.

YES I CAN *SEE* THAT.

RATHER UNFORGIVABLE IN THIS MODERN AGE, ISN'T IT?

'SCUSE ME?

UNFORGIVABLE. THAT WE'D BUILD ELEVATORS AND THEN FORCE SOME OF THE HARD-WORKING MEN OF THE CITY TO BYPASS THEM SIMPLY BECAUSE OF THEIR... *STATION.*

OH, IT'S NOT THAT BAD. USED T' BE I COULD TAKE IT IN STRIDE. I THINK IT'S JUS' THE YEARS CATCHIN' UP WITH ME FINALLY.

YES... WELL, THEY DO CATCH UP WITH US. ALL OF US. SOMETIMES MUCH SOONER THAN WE MIGHT EXPECT.

AIN'T THAT THE TRUTH, SIR. WELL, I'D BETTER BE GETTIN' BACK--

ALL IN GOOD TIME, MY FRIEND. I'M WORRIED ABOUT YOUR WELL-BEING. PLEASE, HAVE A SEAT.

UH... WELL, I DON'T REALLY HAVE ANY MONEY FOR A--

YOU INSULT ME. PART OF MY OATH AS A DOCTOR IS TO GIVE MY SERVICES WHERE *NEEDED* REGARDLESS OF THE BINDING CIRCUMSTANCES. HELP YOURSELF TO A BRANDY?

6

I--THANKS--uh...
THANK YOU.

YOU KNOW, YOU HAVE
A VERY FAMILIAR
FACE.

PEOPLE ARE
ALWAYS TELLIN'
ME THAT.

YES. LITTLE OLDER NOW,
BUT I DO RECOGNIZE
THE FEATURES.

CORRECT ME IF I'M
MISTAKEN, BUT AREN'T
YOU EDDIE ROBINSON?
EDDIE THE ENGINE?

WELL NOW AIN'T YOU
TH' EAGLE EYE? I
DON'T GET RECOGNIZED
MUCH THESE DAYS,
NO SIR.

YEAH...BOXING. THOSE WERE
THE DAYS ALL RIGHT. IF I
HADN'T THROWN OUT MY
BACK, I MIGHT'A GONE FAR...
WHO KNOWS?

AND INSTEAD
YOU'RE NOW JUST
A JUNK RUNNER
FOR THE MOB.

WELL NOW,
I--I MEAN,
I--

IT'S ALL RIGHT,
EDDIE. WE ALL
HAVE OUR LITTLE
MALADIES.

BUT I'M GOING TO GIVE
YOU A PRESCRIPTION THAT,
ONCE FILLED, OUGHT TO
SOLVE ALL OF YOUR
PROBLEMS, INCLUDING
THIS CAREER SLUMP
YOU'RE IN.

HERE.

YOU KNOW,
DOC. YOU
ALL RIGHT.

I MUS' DELIVER
EIGHTY PACKAGES
A DAY, BUT AIN'T
NOBODY TREATS
ME THE WAY YOU
DO.

MM. COUNT
ON IT.

7

11

It's strange how knowledge can come between people.

Familiarity should bring people closer together--

--But the fact that I know something Wes hasn't told me only drives us farther apart.

I'M SORRY, I MUST HAVE BEEN DAYDREAM-ING. WHAT DID YOU SAY?

WELL... ACTUALLY I SAID YOU LOOK A MILLION MILES AWAY. AT LEAST I KNOW MY INTUITION IS STILL INTACT.

YES. THAT'S TRUE.

And yet, if I were to come right out with what I know to be true--

--It could sever our bonds completely.

DIAN? I GET THE FEELING I'VE OFFENDED YOU SOMEHOW.

I'M NOT EXACTLY SURE WHAT I'VE DONE, BUT I WANTED TO GO OUT WITH YOU TO MAKE YOU FEEL GOOD.

WHY DON'T I PROMISE TO NEVER DO IT AGAIN IF YOU PROMISE TO TELL ME WHAT IT IS I'VE DONE?

OH, WESLEY, IT'S NOT THAT. NOT THAT EXACTLY. I JUST FEEL... I FEEL LIKE YOU DON'T REALLY FEEL... COMFORTABLE WITH ME.

DIAN, I FEEL MORE COMFORTABLE WITH YOU THAN I'VE EVER FELT WITH ANYONE IN MY LIFE.

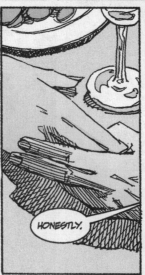

HONESTLY.

YOU KNOW, I THINK I'M JUST MOPEY. LET'S ENJOY THE REST OF OUR MEAL AND WE'LL TALK... OR WHATEVER... LATER.

8

--SO HERE'S THE RUB, VELIKOVSKY IS ONLY PLAYING ONE SHOW IN NEW YORK, AND IT'S A *PRIVATE* SHOW.

OH, THAT'S HORRIBLE.

VERY.

HUMPHRIES? I THINK WE'LL BE HEADING BACK TO THE HOUSE FOR A NIGHTCAP.

VERY GOOD, SIR.

ANYTHING YOU'D LIKE TO TELL ME, HANDSOME?

ONLY THAT I THINK THIS MAY BE THE LONGEST RIDE HOME I'LL EVER HAVE TO LIVE THROUGH.

...WESLEY...

WESLEY...

IS SOMETHING WRONG?

I FEEL...FUNNY. I JUST-- I DON'T THINK THIS IS THE TIME. I'M SORRY, I--

DIAN, THERE'S NOTHING TO BE SORRY ABOUT. THESE THINGS *TAKE* TIME, AND THE MORE TIME THEY TAKE, THE MORE THEY CAN BE SAVORED.

HUMPHRIES? CHANGE IN PLANS. WE'LL BE GOING BY MISS BELMONT'S RESIDENCE.

YES, SIR.

I don't know why this trepidation has such a hold on me.

9

Wesley is so understanding that I'm sure he wouldn't be evasive if I confronted him about his dual life.

But still, if I mattered to him--

--If I truly mattered--

GOOD NIGHT.

GOOD NIGHT, DIAN.

He would tell me of his own volition

Wouldn't he?

I DIDN'T EXPECT YOU BACK SO SOON.

YES, WELL, LIFE'S FULL OF LITTLE SURPRISES LIKE THAT, ISN'T IT?

DIAN? ARE YOU ALL RIGHT? IT'S NOT LIKE YOU TO SNAP.

YOU'RE RIGHT, DADDY. I'M SORRY. IT'S JUST ME, I THINK. I'LL FIGURE IT OUT.

IF YOU NEED ANY HELP, HONEY, I'M ALWAYS HERE.

THANKS, DADDY.

BY THE WAY, I RAN INTO LUCY THIS AFTERNOON. I THINK I MIGHT GO VISIT HER AND HER FAMILY THIS WEEKEND.

DO YOU THINK YOU MIGHT COME ALONG?

OH... I DON'T THINK THAT'S SUCH A GOOD IDEA.

I HAVEN'T REALLY GOTTEN ON WITH BILL SINCE YOUR MOTHER--

--WELL, ANYWAY, YOU ENJOY YOURSELF AND TELL THEM I SAID HELLO, WOULD YOU?

GOODNIGHT, DIAN.

10

HOW'S *THIS* MR. KLEIN?

YEAH... THAT'S FINE, FELLAS.

WHAT'S THE WRITE-UP ON THIS ONE?

SOMEONE FOUND HIM CURLED UP IN AN ALLEY DOWNTOWN.

ONE TOO MANY SHOTS IN THE ARM, I'D GUESS.

WE'LL SEE. IN FORENSIC PATHOLOGY, IT'S ALWAYS BEST NOT TO GET TOO TIED TO ANY PARTICULAR THEORY.

THERE'S ALWAYS THE POSSIBILITY THAT WHAT LOOKS LIKE ONE THING--

--MIGHT TURN OUT TO BE SOMETHING *ELSE* ALTOGETHER.

CHARLES, GO AHEAD AND GET HIM UNDRESSED.

I'VE ALREADY PULLED HIS PERSONALS, MR. KLEIN.

OH, WELL, LET'S HAVE A LOOK. MMM HM. PRETTY COMMON.

WHAT'S *THIS?*

IT APPEARS TO BE A PRE-SCRIPTION--

--FOR, "AN ETERNITY OF REST..."

11

15

NNAHH!

OH, GOOD LORD...

THAT SETTLES IT...

...NO MORE CHOCOLATE PHOSPHATES BEFORE BED.

EXCUSE ME, SIR? I HEARD YOUR CALL. I'M SORRY TO SEE THAT THE DREAMS HAVE RETURNED.

YOU'RE NOT ALONE.

ACTUALLY, SIR, NEITHER ARE YOU. YOU HAD SCHEDULED A LUNCH WITH JUDGE SCHAEFFER WHO IS, IN FACT, ALREADY HERE.

DAMN. UH...SEE IF YOU CAN KEEP THE JUDGE ENTERTAINED, HUMPHRIES. I'LL BE DOWN AS SOON AS POSSIBLE.

SORRY TO HAVE KEPT YOU WAITING SO LONG. SOMETIMES MY MORNING ABLUTIONS STRETCH RIGHT INTO THE AFTERNOON.

YOU KNOW WHAT THEY SAY...

"LATE TO BED, LATE TO RISE, MEANS A LOOK OF LOVE IN THE EYES."

IF ONLY.

YOU'RE LOOKING WELL, WES. DIAN MUST BE JUST WHAT YOU NEEDED.

UH, I DIDN'T KNOW YOU--SHALL WE WALK SOMEWHERE FOR LUNCH?

FINE. IT'S A TERRIFIC DAY OUT.

12

SO HOW LONG HAVE YOU AND LARRY'S ONE-AND-ONLY BEEN DATING, WES?

OH, A WHILE NOW. IT'S REALLY BEEN WORKING OUT QUITE WELL...UNTIL LAST NIGHT.

GET A LITTLE TOO FORWARD, DID YOU?

NO, NOT THAT. I'M NOT SURE WHAT IT WAS. DIAN JUST SEEMED IRRITABLE, DETACHED.

WOMEN GET LIKE THAT, YOU KNOW. DAMNEDEST THING. CATHY GOES OFF ON ME LIKE THAT ALMOST EVERY MONTH, IT SEEMS. WON'T PUT OUT OR SHUT UP.

CATHY? I THOUGHT YOUR WIFE'S NAME WAS ELLEN.

WELL YEAH, HER TOO, NOW THAT YOU MENTION IT.

TAKE MY WORD FOR IT, WES, IF ONE WOMAN IN YOUR LIFE'S TROUBLE, TWO IS ABSOLUTE DAMNATION. DON'T EVER DO IT. OR MAYBE THAT'S THE TROUBLE YOU'RE HAVING--?

NO, NO. NOTHING LIKE THAT.

IT'S JUST THAT,...WELL, ACTUALLY, I THINK I'M JUST UPSET OVER A NIGHTMARE I HAD LAST EVENING. I JUST CAN'T GET IT OUT OF MY HEAD.

WHY DON'T YOU JUST TELL GOOD OLD "DR." SCHAEFFER ABOUT IT? IT HELPS TO TALK THOSE BUGGERS OUT, YOU KNOW.

WELL, I CERTAINLY APPRECIATE THE OFFER, BUT I DON'T LIKE TALKING ABOUT MY DREAMS.

WITH ANYONE.

13

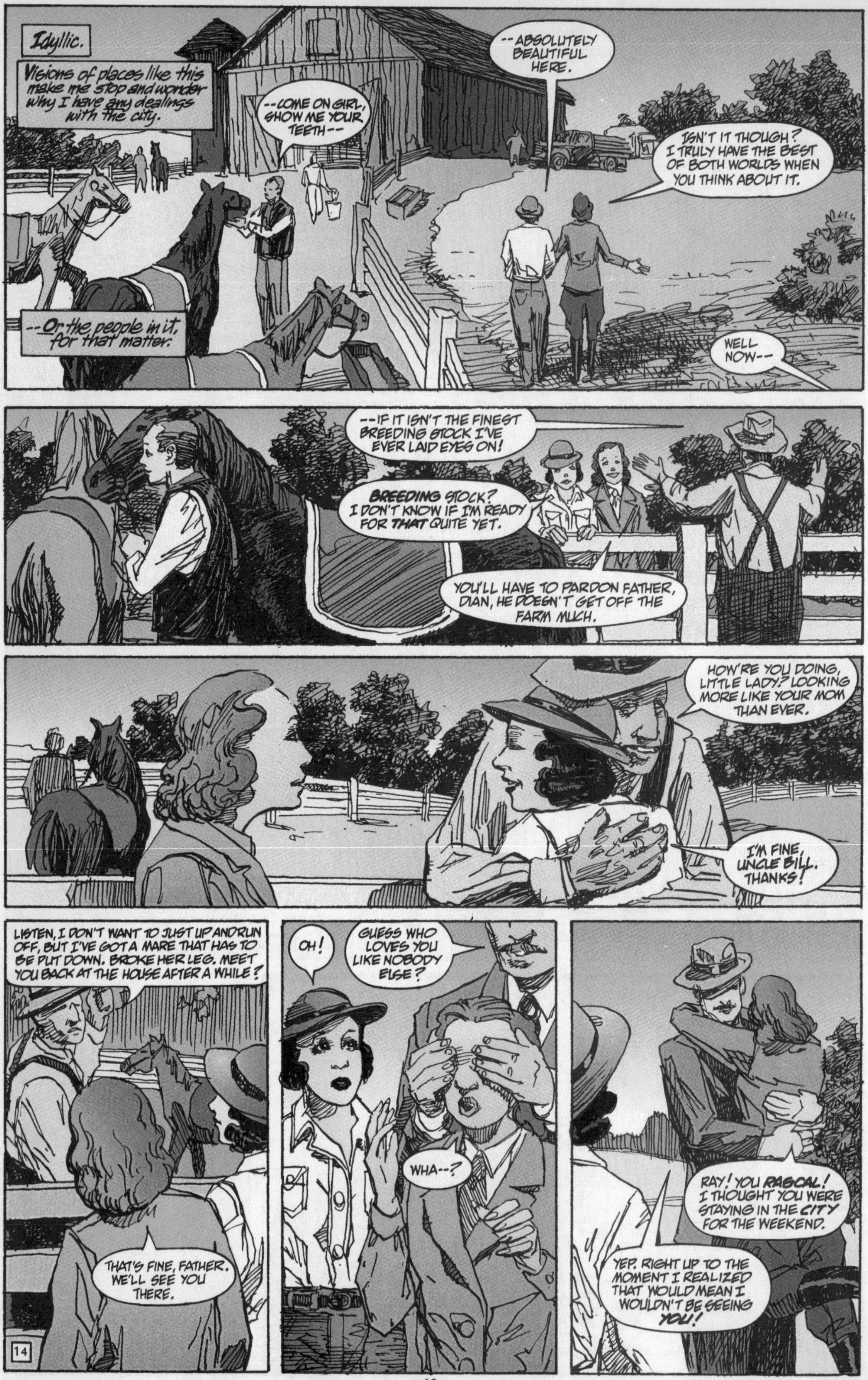
Idyllic.
Visions of places like this make me stop and wonder why I have any dealings with the city.
--COME ON GIRL, SHOW ME YOUR TEETH--
--ABSOLUTELY BEAUTIFUL HERE.
ISN'T IT THOUGH? I TRULY HAVE THE BEST OF BOTH WORLDS WHEN YOU THINK ABOUT IT.
--Or the people in it, for that matter.
WELL NOW--
--IF IT ISN'T THE FINEST BREEDING STOCK I'VE EVER LAID EYES ON!
BREEDING STOCK? I DON'T KNOW IF I'M READY FOR THAT QUITE YET.
YOU'LL HAVE TO PARDON FATHER, DIAN, HE DOESN'T GET OFF THE FARM MUCH.
HOW'RE YOU DOING, LITTLE LADY? LOOKING MORE LIKE YOUR MOM THAN EVER.
I'M FINE, UNCLE BILL. THANKS!
LISTEN, I DON'T WANT TO JUST UP AND RUN OFF, BUT I'VE GOT A MARE THAT HAS TO BE PUT DOWN. BROKE HER LEG. MEET YOU BACK AT THE HOUSE AFTER A WHILE?
THAT'S FINE, FATHER. WE'LL SEE YOU THERE.
14
OH!
GUESS WHO LOVES YOU LIKE NOBODY ELSE?
WHA--?
RAY! YOU RASCAL! I THOUGHT YOU WERE STAYING IN THE CITY FOR THE WEEKEND.
YEP. RIGHT UP TO THE MOMENT I REALIZED THAT WOULD MEAN I WOULDN'T BE SEEING YOU!

DIAN? THIS IS MY MAN, RAYMOND KESSLER.

SO I GATHERED. A PLEASURE TO MEET YOU, RAY.

YOU'RE LUCY'S COUSIN, DIAN?

YES, I--

OF COURSE SHE IS, SILLY. I TOLD YOU THAT. I TOLD HIM THAT, DIAN.

NOW, LUCY, YOU'VE GONE AND MESSED UP MY SMALL TALK. WHATEVER WILL I DO?

AM I BLUSHING?

YOU SILLY BOY!

Look at them.

So in love.

So perfectly, easily in love.

UH... WHERE DID THE TWO OF YOU MEET?

WELL, ACTUALLY I SAW LUCY AT A--

RAYMOND'S BEEN STABLING HIS MOUNT HERE. I ASKED HIM IF HIS HORSE NEEDED A BRUSH DOWN, ONE THING LED TO ANOTHER, AND, WELL...ONE THING LED TO ANOTHER.

RAY'S REALLY BROADENED MY HORIZONS. I EVEN LISTEN TO CLASSICAL MUSIC NOW. TOMORROW WE'RE GOING TO HEAR VLATA-- UH--VALA--

VLADIMIR VELIKOVSKY, YOU MINX.

HE'S PLAYING AT THE AMERICAN MEDICAL ASSOCIATION DINNER.

OH, MY... BOYFRIEND WAS JUST TALKING ABOUT HIM. SAID THAT HE'S A BRILLIANT PIANIST--

JOIN US. IT'S A PRIVATE AFFAIR, BUT I'M ENTITLED TO GUESTS. AND GOD KNOWS MY SON WON'T ATTEND. JUST TELL HIM TO DRESS LIKE A PHYSICIAN.

KRAK

LUCY? I'LL SEE YOU LATER, NO?

OF COURSE YOU WILL, RAY.

I don't know if I should be bemused or envious.

15

--ALL I'M SAYIN', HUBERT, IS YA FOUND THE GUY SMELLIN' LIKE A FRIGGIN' BREWERY. LET'S JUST CHALK IT UP TO BEIN' A DRUNK AN' CALL IT A DAY.

BUT LIEUTENANT, YOU HAVEN'T LET ME TELL YOU ABOUT THE PRESCRIPTION YET.

HE WAS CARRYING A WRITTEN PRESCRIPTION WITH HIM THAT READ, "AN ETERNITY OF REST..." WHAT KIND OF DOCTOR WOULD WRITE SUCH A THING?

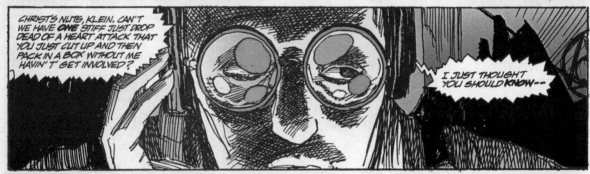

CHRIST'S NUTS, KLEIN. CAN'T WE HAVE **ONE** STIFF JUST DROP DEAD OF A HEART ATTACK THAT YOU JUST CUT UP AND THEN PACK IN A BOX WITHOUT ME HAVIN'T GET INVOLVED?

I JUST THOUGHT YOU SHOULD **KNOW**--

MASTER DODDS?

SORRY TO INTERRUPT, BUT MISS BELMONT IS ON THE LINE. I THOUGHT YOU MIGHT WANT TO--

YES, HUMPHRIES. I'LL TAKE IT. THANK YOU.

HELLO, DIAN?... REALLY? THAT'S FANTASTIC! I'D **LOVE** TO.

...SHOULD BE OUTSTANDING...

...HOPE THEY'RE NOT SERVING FISH...

...RUSSIAN, THOUGH...

PARAMOU

TONIGHT
WELCOME
AMA ANNUAL BANQUET
featuring
VLADIMIR VELIKOVSKY

16

"...SERIOUSLY LODGED IN THE COLON..."

DON'T THINK YOU COULD EVER KEEP THEM ALIVE LONG ENOUGH TO MAKE THE SWITCH...

"...NO, DON'T EAT THAT FISH, IT'LL *KILL* YOU..."

"...WHEN'S THIS GOING TO *START*, ANYWAY..."

WELL *THERE* YOU ARE. I WAS JUST TELLING RAY THAT I THOUGHT YOU MIGHT HAVE DECIDED NOT TO COME.

AND MISS THE LEGENDARY VELIKOVSKY? *NEVER.*

LUCY, RAY? THIS IS MY BOYFRIEND, WESLEY DODDS.

HI, WESLEY. AREN'T *YOU* A CUTIE. THIS IS *MY* BEAU, DR. RAYMOND KESSLER.

PLEASURE TO MEET YOU, WESLEY.

LIKEWISE, RAYMOND. MNN. QUITE A *GRIP* YOU'VE GOT THERE.

I GET A LOT OF PRACTICE AT THESE SORTS OF FUNCTIONS.

DID I HEAR YOU CALL VELIKOVSKY "LEGENDARY"? YOU OBVIOUSLY HAVEN'T HEARD HIM PLAY *LATELY.*

WELL, ACTUALLY, I'VE NEVER HEARD HIM PLAY LIVE AT *ALL.* BUT I DOUBT THAT A MAN OF HIS STATURE COULD *EVER* FALL APPRECIABLY.

17

DON'T PAY TOO MUCH ATTENTION TO DR. TURNER, WESLEY. HE'S BEEN GRUMPY ABOUT *EVERYTHING* SINCE HIS HANDS GAVE OUT.

THAT'S ALL RIGHT, RAYMOND. I LIKE A GOOD SPAR NOW AND AGAIN.

OH, THERE GO THE LIGHTS. WE SHOULD GET OURSELVES IN FOR THE PERFORMANCE.

YOU KNOW, VELIKOVSKY'S HAD A WHOLE *SECOND LIFE* SINCE COMING TO THE STATES.

I'M *REALLY* EXCITED, DIAN. THANKS AGAIN FOR ARRANGING THIS.

YOU CAN THANK ME *LATER*.

Though it would make me happier to have you tell me about your second life.

THANK YOU.

CLAP CLAP CLAP CLAP

To explain why a man as cultured as yourself--

--As secure as yourself--

--Would feel the need to dress up at night in that outrageous getup.

Why do you live behind that mask of yours, Wesley?

18

22

HM?

"HM?" WHAT KIND OF A REACTION IS THAT FOR THE "GREAT VELIKOVSKY?"

OH, I WAS JUST THINKING ABOUT DR. TURNER'S COMMENT EARLIER--

--MAYBE VELIKOVSKY HAS PASSED HIS PRIME.

YOU THINK THE MAESTRO SHOULD RETIRE--

WELL...

YES, VELL, THE CZAR VAS, AT THET TIME...

EXCUSE ME, SORRY TO INTERRUPT, BUT I HAD TO GIVE YOU MY CONGRATULATIONS. A TRULY INSPIRED PERFORMANCE, MR. VELIKOVSKY.

EH?

DR. RAYMOND KESSLER.

THENK YOU VERY MUCH, DR. KESSLER.

UH, THANK YOU.

I HOPE YOU'RE FINDING THE NEW YORK CLIMATE HOSPITABLE.

YES, VELL, IS BETTER THAN THE SIBERIAN.

19

23

MMM, YES. IT *DID* LOOK LIKE HE WAS IN PAIN AT TIMES. PITY.

PROBABLY ARTHRITIS, OR MAYBE BURSITIS. STILL A NICE ENOUGH PERFORMANCE. DIDN'T YOU THINK, LUCY?

Hmm?

OH, *LOOK* AT THAT, I SEEM TO HAVE SPILLED SOMETHING ON MYSELF. EXCUSE ME FOR A MOMENT, LADIES...RAY.

HURRY BACK, WES.

NO NEED TO WORRY. IT'S MINOR.

...COULDN'T BE SODA... HAD TO BE GRAVY...

YOU KNOW THE SELTZER YILL TAKE THET OUT.

REALLY?

DAH. VAS MY WIFE'S REMEDY.

I'VE BEEN A *BIG* FOLLOWER OF YOUR WORK, MR. VELIKOVSKY.

Hmm, VELL, I HOPE YOU ENJOYED THE CONCERT THIS NIGHT. A FEW STUMBLES, BUT I EM AN OLD MAN NOW.

AN OLD MAN WITH MUSSED HAIR TO COMB--

--*eh?*

A NOTE TO YOURSELF YOU'D FORGOTTEN? I'M *ALWAYS* DOING THAT.

NO. IS SOMEONE'S IDEA OF A JOKE... A *BAD* JOKE.

20

24

EXCUSE ME.

Permanant Retirement

--AND GOOD SEEING *YOU* AGAIN, RAY. YOU TAKE CARE OF MY COUSIN, NOW!

NO NEED TO WORRY ABOUT *THAT*, DIAN. GOODNIGHT.

GOODNIGHT. COME ON, RAY, LET'S *GO!*

WELL THAT WAS SPIRITED, BUT I'M GLAD TO FINALLY BE ALONE WITH YOU. I WAS HOPING WE--

ACTUALLY, DIAN, THOUGH I HATE TO DO IT, I'M AFRAID I'M GOING TO HAVE TO CALL IT A NIGHT.

IT'S ANOTHER EARLY MORNING FOR ME TOMORROW, BUT LET'S *DO* GET TOGETHER IN THE EVENING AND FINISH THIS DISCUSSION.

WESLEY--

NO, DON'T WORRY ABOUT ME, I'LL JUST CATCH A CAB. GOODNIGHT!

An early morning or a late night?

21

25

UNHH! CHRIST!

NOT NOW. *PLEASE* MY FRIENDS, NOT AGAIN TONIGHT--

RACHMANINOFF SUITS YOU, VLADIMIR VELIKOVSKY. IT IS DARK AND BROODING... LIKE THE NIGHT.

WHAT? GOOD LORD! HAVE YOU COME TO KILL ME?

22

THERE IS NOT MUCH MUSIC LEFT IN THESE HANDS, I AM AFRAID. ARTHRITIS. THE BRANDY HELPS, BUT LESS SO EACH DAY.

I AM HERE NEITHER FOR YOUR LIFE NOR YOUR MUSIC, BUT ONLY TO INQUIRE ABOUT YOUR PERFORMANCE AT THE AMERICAN MEDICAL ASSOCIATION DINNER.

PLEASE... ASK YOUR QUESTIONS.

I HAVE REASON TO BELIEVE THAT YOU RECEIVED A PRESCRIPTION NOTICE BEFORE YOU PLAYED. IS THIS SO?

THAT WAS FROM YOU? I THOUGHT IT A JOKE. "PERMANENT RETIREMENT." A BIT *DRAMATIC* DON'T YOU THINK?

THE NOTE WAS NOT OF MY DEVISING. I SEEK ITS PRACTITIONER--

OH! CHRIST! UNNH--!

VELIKOVSKY! YOUR FATE IS UPON YOU--

UNHHH! AAAAH! HURRF!

--QUICKLY, YOU MUST TELL ME WHO GAVE YOU THE PRESCRIPTION. WHAT DID HE LOOK LIKE?

BLACK--

HE WAS NEGRO?

--AND WHITE... ALWAYS...BLACK AND WHI--

23

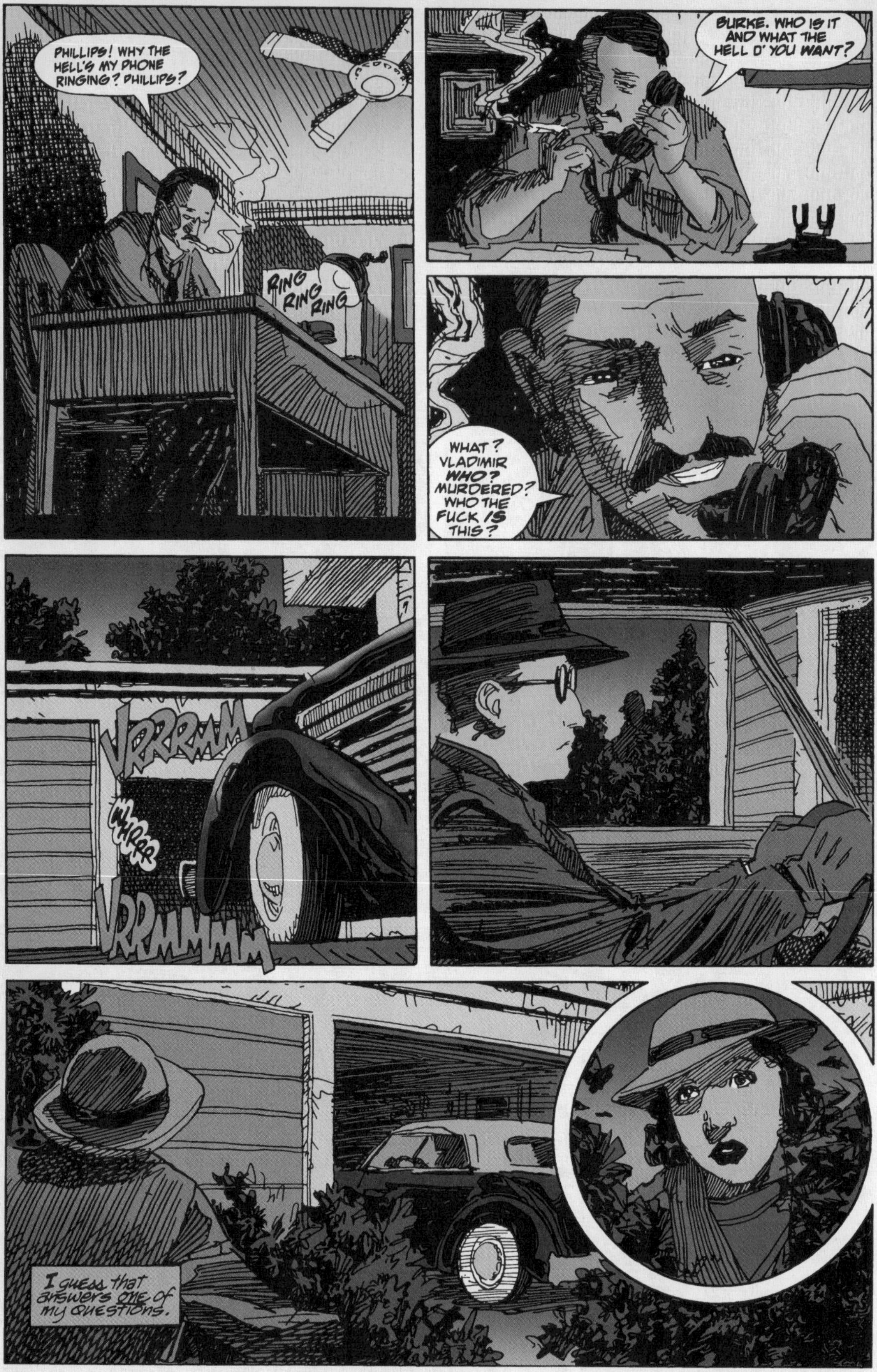
PHILLIPS! WHY THE HELL'S MY PHONE RINGING? PHILLIPS?
RING RING RING
BURKE. WHO IS IT AND WHAT THE HELL D' YOU WANT?
WHAT? VLADIMIR WHO? MURDERED? WHO THE FUCK IS THIS?
VRRRAM
WHRRR
VRRMMMMM
I guess that answers ONE of my questions.

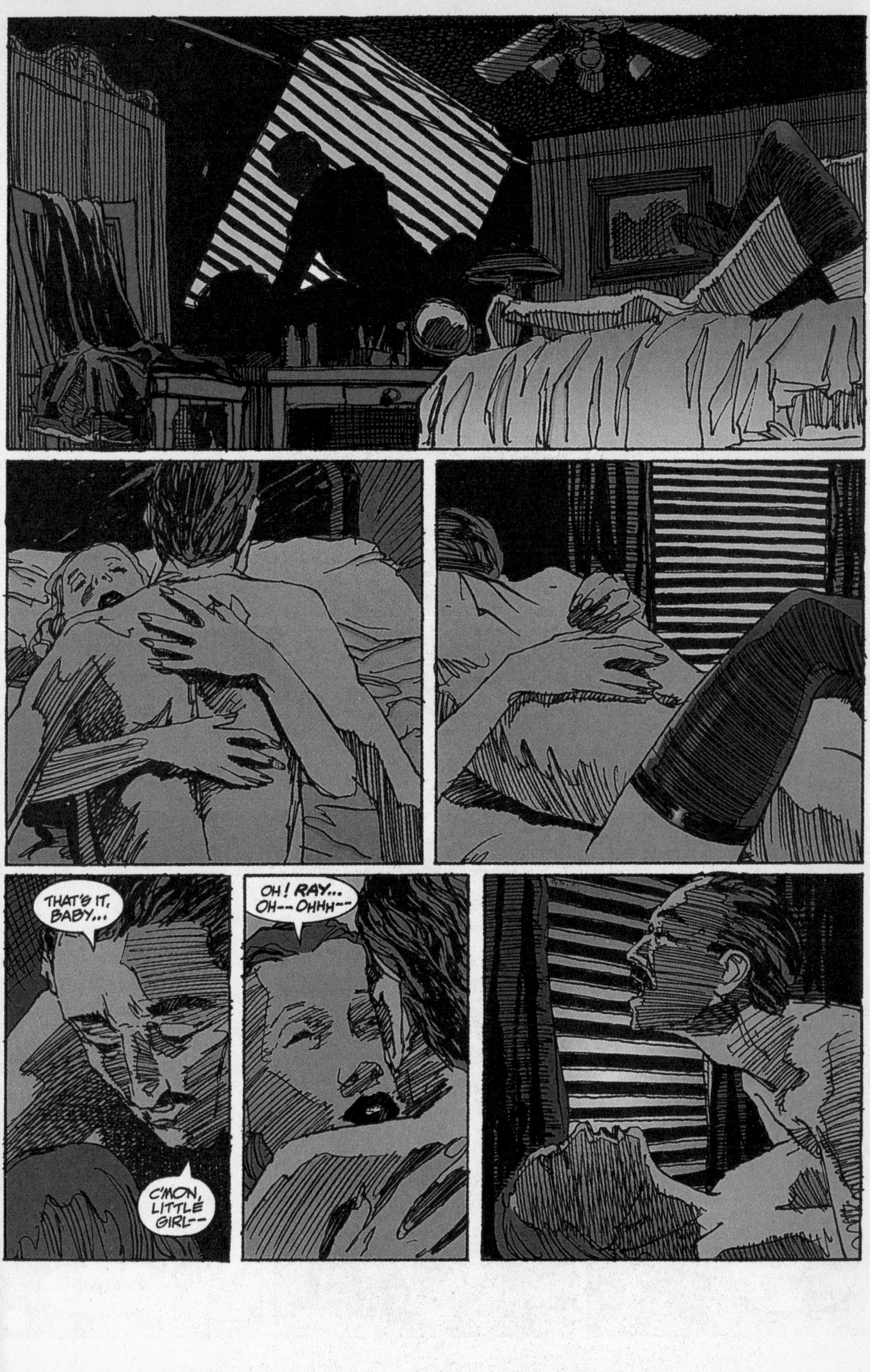
THAT'S IT, BABY...
C'MON, LITTLE GIRL--
OH! RAY... OH-- OHHH--

FFLTCH

RAY?

HOW YOU HOLDIN' UP, BABY?

JESUS, I *HOPE* SO.

THAT WAS *SO GOOD.* I REALLY FELT YOU IN ME.

YOU KNOW WHAT I MEAN, TIGER.

LUCY... WHAT WOULD YOU SAY IF I TOLD YOU I WANTED TO GET YOU PREGNANT?

IS THAT A PROPOSAL OR A PROPOSITION?

WHAT IF IT'S *BOTH?*

COME HERE, BABY.

AGAIN? *ALREADY?* RAY, YOU--

THAT'S RIGHT, I *AM.*

WELL, OKAY... I MEAN, YES, DARL--

OH RAY! P-PLEASE, RAY... OHHH...YES, RAY...

NNNNNNNH...

What happens when you get what you want?

I've convinced myself more than ever that Wesley is secretly the Sandman, but NOW what?

Do I try to understand Wesley's evasiveness?

Do I confront him?

Do I leave him altogether? That would probably be the safest thing.

Maybe I should just go to sleep.

But what good would that do? I just know I won't be able to rest tonight.

I'll be up and awake. Wondering.

Wondering and worrying about you, Wes...

Afraid that you might be hurt...

Or worse...

Afraid that I may never see you again...

...Afraid that I will.

Why is this so difficult?

...AND WHAT DOES THIS MEAN...?

DR. DEATH
act two

I DON'T *KNOW*, LIEUTENANT. HE'S BEEN DEAD A WHILE, NOW. I WISH I COULD HAVE SEEN THE BODY *SOONER*.

WELL, *HOWEVER* YOU GOT THE TIP, IT'S NEARLY NOON--

--AND I'D SAY THIS MAN HAS BEEN DEAD SINCE LATE LAST NIGHT.

WE'VE ALREADY LOST AN AWFUL LOT OF VALUABLE INFORMATION. I'M NOT EVEN SURE IF I'LL BE ABLE TO--

...NAH, I'M TELLIN' YA, I WAS LIKE VALENTINO OR SOMETHIN'. I COULDN'T STOP--

COULDN'T STOP TALKIN' *BULLSHIT*, YA MEAN...

YEAH, WELL I WISH WE DIDN'T HAVE TO SEE A BODY LOOKIN' LIKE THAT AT *ALL*, BUT YOU DON'T ALWAYS GET WHAT YOU *WANT!*

WE GOT AN ANONYMOUS TIP FROM SOME BASTARD WHO TOLD US THIS VOLLI-WHATSIS GUY WAS MUR-DERED, BUT HE DIDN'T GIVE US AN *ADDRESS*.

LOOK, HUBERT. IT TOOK ME A WHILE T' EVEN FIND OUT WHO THIS GUY *WAS.*

LET ALONE *WHERE* HE WAS.

EXCUSE THE HELL OUTTA ME IF EVERY MURDER IN TOWN DOESN'T COME WITH A PERSONALIZED INVITATION AND A MAP.

IT WAS AN ANONYMOUS TIP FOR CRYIN' OUT LOUD.

YOU THINK *YOU* CAN DO BETTER? BE MY FUCKIN' GUEST.

THIS WAS AN ANONYMOUS CALL?

YEAH, BUT I GOT AN IDEA WHO IT WAS.

WELL, *WHOEVER* IT WAS, ONE THING IS *CERTAIN*--

--THIS BUILDUP ON HIS FACE DIDN'T COME FROM PLAY-ING STRAUSS.

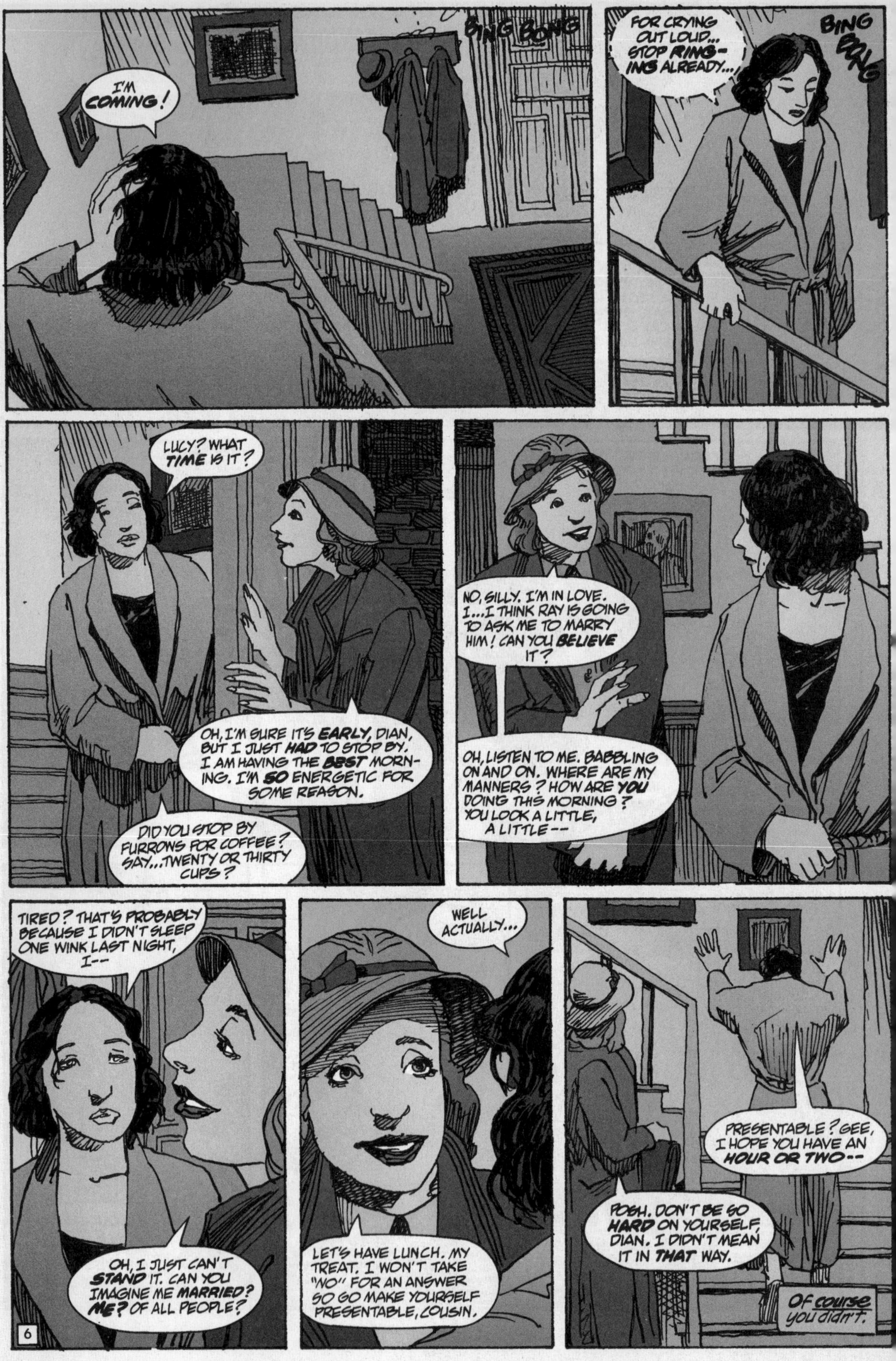
I'M COMING!
BING BONG
FOR CRYING OUT LOUD... STOP RINGING ALREADY...!
BING BONG
LUCY? WHAT TIME IS IT?
OH, I'M SURE IT'S EARLY, DIAN, BUT I JUST HAD TO STOP BY. I AM HAVING THE BEST MORNING. I'M SO ENERGETIC FOR SOME REASON.
DID YOU STOP BY FURROWS FOR COFFEE? SAY...TWENTY OR THIRTY CUPS?
NO, SILLY. I'M IN LOVE. I...I THINK RAY IS GOING TO ASK ME TO MARRY HIM! CAN YOU BELIEVE IT?
OH, LISTEN TO ME. BABBLING ON AND ON. WHERE ARE MY MANNERS? HOW ARE YOU DOING THIS MORNING? YOU LOOK A LITTLE, A LITTLE--
TIRED? THAT'S PROBABLY BECAUSE I DIDN'T SLEEP ONE WINK LAST NIGHT, I--
OH, I JUST CAN'T STAND IT. CAN YOU IMAGINE ME MARRIED? ME? OF ALL PEOPLE?
6
WELL ACTUALLY...
LET'S HAVE LUNCH. MY TREAT. I WON'T TAKE "NO" FOR AN ANSWER SO GO MAKE YOURSELF PRESENTABLE, COUSIN.
PRESENTABLE? GEE, I HOPE YOU HAVE AN HOUR OR TWO--
POSH. DON'T BE SO HARD ON YOURSELF, DIAN. I DIDN'T MEAN IT IN THAT WAY.
Of course you didn't.

--DON'T KNOW WHAT IT IS, I JUST FEEL BLUE.

WHAT ABOUT THIS *BOYFRIEND* OF YOURS?

PARK WAY DINER

WESLEY? WHAT DO YOU *MEAN*? HE'S FINE...I GUESS.

YOU *GUESS*? WHAT KIND OF ANSWER IS THAT? I MEAN, I'M NOT TRYING TO SAY HE ISN'T *SWEET*. IT'S NOT *THAT*--

--BUT AT THE DINNER THE OTHER NIGHT, HE JUST SEEMED...WELL, YOU'RE SO VIBRANT AND YOUNG, AND HE'S...WELL, HE'S --

NOT A MOVIE STAR? LUCY, WESLEY AND I MAY *LOOK* WORLDS APART, BUT WE'RE REALLY VERY CLOSE. WE'RE OF THE SAME MIND ON A *NUMBER* OF THINGS.

WELL, IT WASN'T REALLY HIS *MIND* I WAS THINKING ABOUT.

I MEAN, YOU'RE A YOUNG *WOMAN*, LIKE ME. WE HAVE CERTAIN...*NEEDS*. AND RAY... WELL, LET'S JUST SAY HE DE-FINITELY HAS WHAT I NEED.

OH *REALLY*?

WELL, I... THAT'S...UH--

AND YOU KNOW, I *DID* GROW UP ON A *HORSE* FARM AFTER ALL.

I CALL IT THE EMPIRE STATE BUILDING.

>snicker<

7

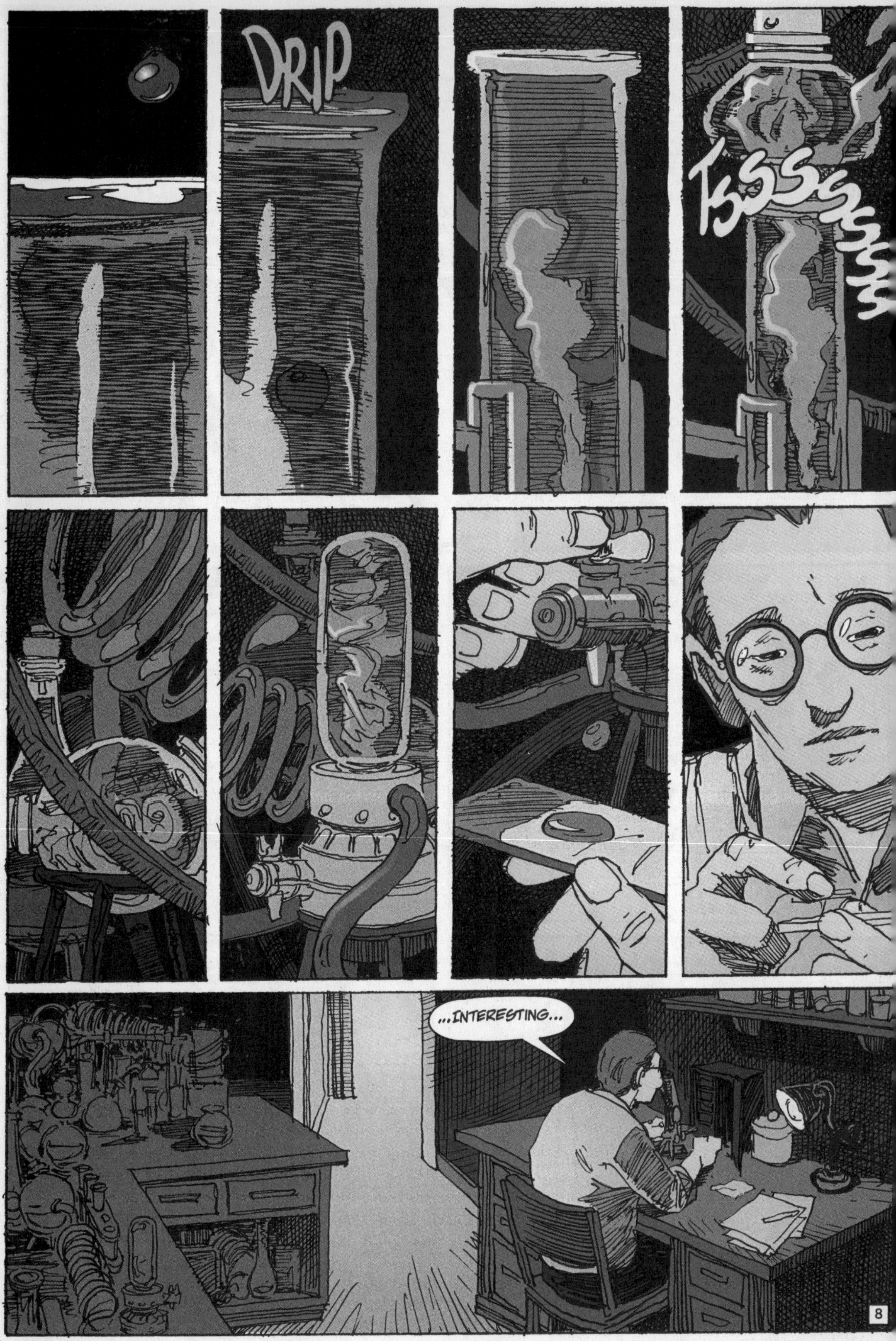
DRIP
TSSSSSSSS
...INTERESTING...
8

--INTERESTING.

WHAT IN THE WORLD ARE YOU DOING WITH *THAT* IN YOUR STOMACH, VLADIMIR?

ACID-BASE REACTIONS AREN'T VERY PLEASURABLE GASTRO-INTESTINAL COCKTAILS.

HERE WE ARE...*uh-huh*... GOODNESS ME.

SORRY TO HAVE TO TELL YOU THIS--

--BUT THE INTENSITY OF THE DOINGS IN YOUR GUT INDICATE THAT YOU HAD TO SOMEHOW CONSUME HUGE AMOUNTS OF THE BASE FOLLOWED BY THE ACID.

THAT MEANS I'M GOING TO NEED YOUR *LIVER* TOO, MY FRIEND.

BUT IF YOU'LL PARDON THE INDISCRETION--

--WE *MAY* JUST GET TO THE BOTTOM OF THIS.

9

Lucy is quite the bundle of surprises.

Not only is she dating an older man...

--but she's apparently deeply involved with him sexually as well.

And I thought Wesley and I were adventurous.

But that's our relationship all over, isn't it, Wesley?

Committed, but not terribly advanced.

HELLO, WES?

DIAN! HELLO. IT'S GOOD TO HEAR YOUR VOICE. I WAS STARTING TO GO A LITTLE STIR CRAZY SITTING HERE AT MY DESK.

WELL THAT'S JUST ACES, BECAUSE I WAS ABOUT TO INVITE YOU OUT FOR AN EARLY DINNER...IF YOU'RE INTERESTED--?

INTERESTED, BUT UNAVAILABLE. I'VE BEEN UP WORKING ALL NIGHT AND I'M STILL NOT QUITE DONE WITH--

WES!

YOU-- YOU'RE ALWAYS BUSY. WHAT ABOUT FINDING TIME FOR ME? FOR US?

I--I'M SORRY, DIAN. I THOUGHT YOU UNDER-STOOD.

MY WORK DEMANDS A LOT OF TIME. I'M SURE YOU'LL SEE HOW HARD IT IS TO MANAGE THINGS WHEN YOU'RE NO LONGER LIVING WITH YOUR FATHER. IT'S--

AND JUST WHAT THE--WHAT THE HELL IS THAT SUPPOSED TO MEAN?

YOU THINK I'M JUST SOME IDLE DEBUTANTE. IS THAT IT?

I--NO, DIAN, OF COURSE NOT. THAT'S NOT WHAT I MEANT TO SAY AT ALL, I JUST--

10

I think it's *EXACTLY* what you meant to say--

--BUT AS FAR AS *I'M* CONCERNED, YOU CAN JUST TELL IT TO YOUR *WORK!* GOOD BYE!

DUMB, WESLEY... VERY DUMB.

--NO THANK YOU, DRIVER, I DON'T WANT MY BOYFRIEND TO KNOW HOW I GOT HERE, HE ISN'T EXPECTING ME.

THANKS ANYHOW! THE EXTRA QUARTER IS FOR YOU!

-- THE *FUCK* YOU WILL!

...RAY--?

YOU ARE THE MOST *UNGRATEFUL* BASTARD TO EVER SET FOOT ON THIS EARTH, YOU KNOW THAT?

LIKE FATHER LIKE SON, eh, RAYMOND?

THAT'S IT--!

OH DEAR.

BING BONG

WHO THE HELL IS-- UH--

HI, RAY.

LUCY. WHAT A... SURPRISE.

I HOPE I'M NOT INTERRUPTING ANYTHING?

UH...NO, NO, COME IN...

I WAS JUST HAVING A TALK WITH MY SON, ROMAN? THIS IS LUCY.

A PLEASURE TO MEET Y--

GOOD GOING, DAD. AT LEAST THIS ONE IS ALMOST MY AGE.

YOUNG MAN!

YOU HAD BETTER SHOW THIS LADY SOME RESPECT AND APOLOGIZE THIS INSTANT.

YOU ALWAYS SAID I LET YOU DOWN--

--JUST CONSIDER THIS ANOTHER EXAMPLE.

ROMAN!

LEAVE ME ALONE!

SLAM

LUCY, I--

DON'T LET IT GET YOU DOWN, HONEY. FAMILIES ARE TOUGH TO--

FORGET IT. LET'S PUT IT BEHIND US. I'VE GOT A SURPRISE FOR YOU.

SOMETHING THAT WILL LIVEN THIS DISMAL ENCOUNTER.

TICKETS TO A SHOW!

12

KLEIN?

KLEIN!

--EH?

OH! IT'S *YOU.* PLEASE, DON'T SHOOT ME! REMEMBER MY ALLER--

SHOOT YA? WHAT TH' HELL'RE YOU TALKIN' ABOUT?

OH... BURKE. I'M SORRY. I THOUGHT YOU WERE... SOMEONE *ELSE.*

YEAH, WELL, I'M NOT. WHAT YA GOT FOR ME ON THAT STIFFED RUSSKIE?

OH, VELIKOVSKY... YES. STRANGE CASE.

FROM WHAT I CAN GATHER, HE DIED FROM AN ACUTE ACID-BASE REACTION IN HIS STOMACH.

SHOULD I BRING MY OWN GODDAMN TRANSLATOR OR YOU GOT ONE HIDDEN IN THE BROOM CLOSET?

SORRY. ESSENTIALLY, VELIKOVSKY ATE OR DRANK TWO THINGS WHICH WHEN MIXED, BOILED HIS STOMACH AND SUFFOCATED HIM BY BLISTERING HIS ESOPHAGUS.

EVEN MORE STRANGE IS THAT I BELIEVE THIS TO BE THE *SAME* CAUSE OF DEATH FOR EDDIE THE ENGINE ROBINSON.

SAME CAUSE? NAH. NO LINK WHATSOEVER BETWEEN THE DEFECTOR AND THE COON, KLEIN.

GUESS THAT'S WHY *I'M* THE DETECTIVE AND YOU'RE THE GRAVE ROBBER. KEEP WORKING, I'LL CHECK BACK WITH YOU LATER.

13

SLAM

KOONG, HUH? WHAT DO YOU THINK OF JEWS?

HUBERT KLEIN--

BURKE HAS GONE. I LISTENED AS YOU SPOKE TO HIM. I TOO BELIEVE THESE KILLINGS TO BE CONNECTED.

YOU?!

THIS IS A NOTE GIVEN TO ONE OF THE MEN BEFORE HIS DEATH.

I'LL BET I KNOW WHAT THIS SAYS.

EDDIE ROBINSON HAD ONE, TOO.

HMM, ISN'T THAT STRANGE? SAME M.O. BUT A DIFFERENT MESSAGE. AND THIS WEIRD SYMBOL...

LOOKS TO BE STAMPED RATHER THAN PRINTED.

THE REACTION THAT KILLED VELIKOVSKY WOULD SUGGEST A CHEMIST?

UM...POSSIBLY, BUT CHEMISTS DON'T ISSUE PRESCRIPTIONS. MORE LIKELY A PHYSICIAN.

A LEFT-HANDED PHYSICIAN FROM THE SLANT OF BOTH WRITINGS.

YOU ARE A MAN OF KEEN SENSES, HUBERT KLEIN.

SHOULD YOU NEED TO CONTACT ME AGAIN, USE THE PERSONAL COLUMNS OF THE TIMES.

14

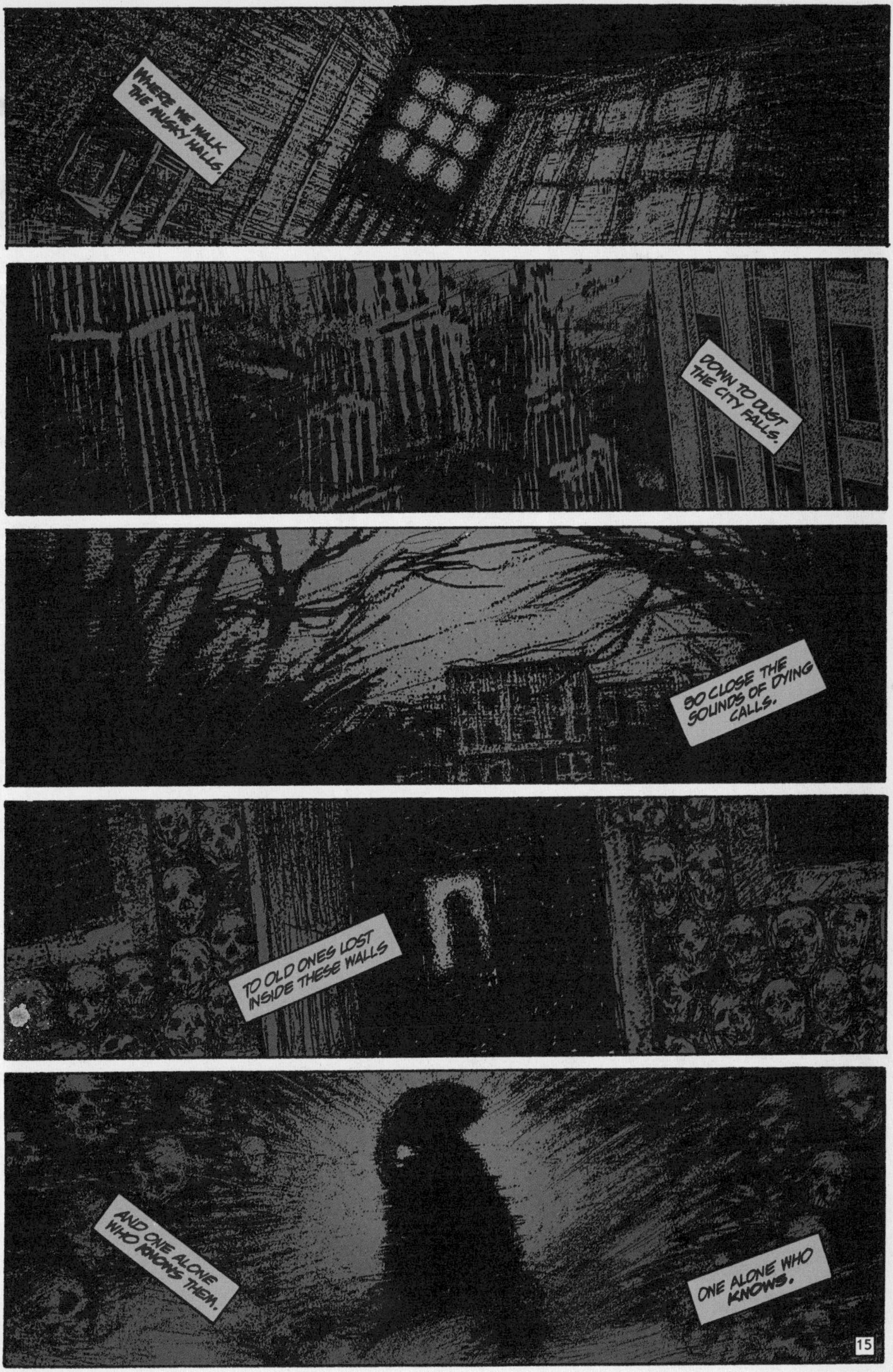
WHERE WE WALK THE MUSKY HALLS.
DOWN TO DUST THE CITY FALLS.
SO CLOSE THE SOUNDS OF DYING CALLS.
TO OLD ONES LOST INSIDE THESE WALLS
AND ONE ALONE WHO KNOWS THEM.
ONE ALONE WHO KNOWS.
15

WESLEY--?

What an awful dream.

OH...OH MY GOODNESS.

I haven't felt this... scared since my mother passed away.

I never have dreams like that. What could have caused such horrible visions?

Minnie's mother is a spiritualist. Maybe I should call her and ask her what it all means.

Oh, get a grip on yourself, Dian.

You just had a bad day and a bad night was sure to follow.

The only thing you need is to clear up all of those oppressive thoughts swirling around in your head.

TONIGHT ONLY CLACKIE BROWN

--SO HE TELLS THE DANCER, "NO, BUT THOSE AREN'T MY TOES!" Heh heh!

HEH...GET IT? TOES...?

ALL RIGHT, WELL...DID I TELL YOU THE ONE ABOUT THE WAITER? GOOD!

16

SO, THIS WAITER IS CALLED OVER BY THIS GENTLEMAN--

--AND THE GENTLEMAN SAYS, "WAITER, THERE'S A FLY IN MY SOUP!"

AND THE WAITER SAYS--GET *THIS* HE SAYS--

"THAT MUST BE THE ONE THE BROOKLYN *DODGERS* ARE LOOKING FOR!" HEH HEH!

THAT'S ALL FOR NOW, LADIES AND GERMS! GOOOOOOOD NIGHT!

STOP RIGHT *THERE*, YOU LITTLE CREEP.

SOMETHING WRONG, MR. TROWER? YOU LOOK *ANGRY*--

AT LEAST I DON'T LOOK *BORED* LIKE THE AUDIENCE. YOU TOLD ME YOU HAD ALL NEW JOKES, YOU LITTLE *SONUVABITCH.* I WAS GIVIN' YOU A *BREAK* HERE.

WELL SURE, I *HAD* NEW MATERIAL, BUT THAT WAS A TOUGH CROWD... UH... I DECIDED THE *CLASSICS* WOULD FLY BETTER. YOU KNOW...

WHAT ABOUT ALL THEM SKINNY JOKES? HUH? AT LEAST *THOSE* USED T' GET LAUGHS.

AHHH... NOBODY *LIKES* THOSE JOKES ANYMORE. THEY WANNA THINK THE DEPRESSION'S OVER--

LOOK, CLACKIE. WE BOTH KNOW THE DEAL HERE. YOU JUST AIN'T GOT IT ANYMORE. WHAT THE SMACK DIDN'T *TEAR* OUTTA YOU, THE *BOOZE* PICKLED.

EITHER WAY, I CAN'T JUST SUPPORT YOUR PATHETIC PUSS NO MORE. THERE'S THE DOOR--

17

DON'T LET IT HIT YA IN THE ASS ON YOUR WAY OUT.

PACKAGE FOR CLACKIE BROWN?

RIGHT HERE, YOUNG MAN. A GIFT FROM MY ADMIRING PUBLIC?

GEEZ, MISTER. I DON'T KNOW.

WELL LET ME GIVE YOU A TIP...DON'T TAKE ANY WOODEN NICKELS! HEH HEH.

FUNNY.

COMEDY IS MY LIFE, KID.

LET'S SEE... WHAT HAVE WE HERE...?

HMM...STIFF BELT'S JUST WHAT I NEED.

HUH...?

Your final curtain call

DON'T KNOW HOW YOU KNEW THAT, MY FRIEND, BUT I'M NOT COMPLAINING.

HARLEM FIRST CHURCH OF CHRIST

CLAK

18

"JESUS DONE TOL' ME-- ♪ HE'S COMIN' HOME--"

"--JESUS DONE TOL' ME-- ♪ HE'S COMIN' HOME--♪"

MIRANDA ROBINSON?

--JESUS--!

YOU STAY RIGHT THERE OR I'M GONNA LAY YOU OUT.

I AM NOT HERE TO HURT YOU. I HAVE COME FOR INFORMATION REGARDING YOUR BROTHER, EDDIE.

WELL... I DONE TALKED TO THE POLICE AN' I AIN'T GOT NOTHIN' MORE TO TELL NO SPOOK WORKIN' WITH 'EM!

I AM NOT WITH THE POLICE. BUT, I DO INTEND TO SEE YOUR BROTHER'S KILLER BROUGHT TO JUSTICE.

MISTER, I LOVED EDDIE. I DID. BUT HE DID STUFF TO THE GONNA HAVE TO EXPLAIN TO THE LORD ALMIGHTY JESUS HIS-SELF. DIDN'T NOBODY KILL EDDIE BUT EDDIE.

MISS ROBINSON... YOUR BROTHER WAS MURDERED. I CAN ASSURE YOU OF THAT.

MURDERED? EDDIE?

YES.

OH, EDDIE. I'M SORRY. I DIDN'T MEAN YOU NO DISRESPECT.

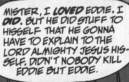

BUT THEM DRUGS YOU GOT FOR DELIVERIN' THEM PACKAGES...

...I TOL' YOU THAT WEREN'T GONNA COME TO NO GOOD.

MAY THE LORD JESUS CHRIST HAVE MERCY ON YOUR SOUL, EDDIE--

AN' MERCY ON MINE TOO.

19

GETTA LOAD A *THIS* PLACE. *SHEESH!* SOME PEOPLE GOT IT *ROUGH.*

MAY I *HELP* YOU?

SURE, BUB. GOT A PIANO HERE FOR A... "*WESLY DOBBS?*"

A PIANO? THERE MUST BE SOME *MISTAKE.*

NOPE. LOOK RIGHT THERE. THAT'S YOUR ADDRESS AIN'T IT?

WELL YES, IT IS. BUT I CAN *ASSURE* YOU THAT MASTER DODDS HAS *NOT* ORDERED A PIANO--

MUSTA DID. I'M LOOKIN' AT IT RIGHT THERE--

NOW SEE *HERE.* YOU CAN'T JUST LEAVE A PIANO--

I suppose I should feel guilty...a little bit.

ISN'T THERE SOMEONE I COULD *PHONE* TO TALK TO ABOUT THIS--?

But then again, this is what you yourself do, isn't it, Wes?

Behave in a bold fashion to arrive at the answers you need.

Well, what's good for the gander...

Besides, what other choice do I have?

I remember once, when I was in Catholic school--

--I brought my mother's ring for show and tell.

At the end of the day, it was missing from my desk.

Someone told me that Ruda, who was my best friend in the whole world, had taken it.

I was crestfallen, but I asked her if she had it.

She looked me straight in the eye and said, "Of course not, Dian. We're best friends. How could you think that?"

Two weeks later I found the ring in her jewelry box.

I took it and I never spoke to her again. We both knew why.

How much better it would have been if she had just told me the truth when I asked--

SLAM

SHOOT!

CH-CHOK

RRRING

DODDS RESIDENCE... HELLO? IS ANY- ONE THERE?

--and not forced me to find it on my own.

21

ROBERT LI! N.Y.U. MUST BE TREATING ITS STATISTICS PROFESSORS *VERY* WELL THESE DAYS.

WESLEY! YOU'RE LOOKING FIT!

ME? YOU STILL LOOK THE *SAME* AS YOU DID THE DAY I MET YOU AT THE NATIONAL HONOR SOCIETY MEETING.

IT IS THE CHINESE IN ME. IT KEEPS ME *YOUTHFUL*.

I WAS IN THE NEIGHBORHOOD AND WONDERED IF YOU STILL HAUNT THE EDISON AT LUNCH.

STATISTICALLY SOLID, MY FRIEND.

I'D HEARD YOU MOVED BACK TO TOWN. HOW'S IT FEEL TO BE BACK IN THE BIG APPLE?

NOSTALGIC. SPEAKING OF WHICH... MENTAL CHALLENGE.

HA! YOU REMEMBER.

I CHALLENGE YOU, SOCIETY BROTHER, TO COMPILE A LIST OF ALL THE... UH... *LEFT-HANDED PHYSICIANS* ON MANHATTAN ISLAND.

SIMPLICITY ITSELF. I CHALLENGE *YOU*, SOCIETY BROTHER, TO... *MEMORIZE* TWO COMPLETE PAGES OF THE *NEW YORK TIMES*.

I MAY HAVE CHOSEN THE WRONG DAY TO *CHALLENGE* YOU, ROBERT! THAT'S A *TOUGH* ONE.

WE'LL MEET AGAIN, SAY THE DAY AFTER TOMORROW? WINNER BUYS NOT *ONLY* DRINKS AND DINNER, BUT TWO TICKETS TO THE *OPERA* AS WELL.

ACCEPTED. LUNCH?

LET'S.

Nothing.

22

I don't believe that there was no trace of... of *anything*.

I can't be imagining all this... can I?

There are such things as coincidences after all—

YOU LOOK LIKE YOU'RE ON ANOTHER WORLD.

LUCY?

IN THE FLESH. I JUST DROPPED BY TO INTRODUCE RAY TO UNCLE LARRY. YOU KNOW... MEET THE *FAMILY* AND ALL.

OF COURSE. I'M SORRY, I JUST DIDN'T *SEE* YOU THERE, I'VE BEEN A BIT PREOCCUPIED TODAY.

WELL I HOPE HE'S TALL, DARK AND HANDSOME! >giggle<

NOW, LUCY. DON'T TEASE. WESLEY IS A CHARMING CHAP... IN HIS OWN WAY.

uh, LISTEN, WHY DON'T I JUST GO AND SEE WHAT'S KEEPING DADDY?

WE'LL BE RIGHT HERE WAITING.

SURE THING.

DADDY?

23

--NO, NO. I'LL COME DOWN TO THE *STATION.* I'M TRYING TO KEEP THESE THINGS AWAY FROM THE HOUSE... *YOU* KNOW...

...NO, NOTHING LIKE *THAT,* IT'S JUST THAT SHE GOT A LITTLE TOO CLOSE TO THE LAST SITUATION AND--

EXACTLY...EXACTLY... SHE *IS* MY LITTLE GIRL--

"Daddy's little girl."

--RA-AAAY! STOP IT! >giggle<

WHAT IF DIAN COMES BACK?

WE'LL HEAR HER.

How many fathers really know what their little girls are up to?

YOU'RE SOOOOO BAD.

Or would really want to know what lurks inside their...I guess I should say "hearts."

Then again...maybe Lucy's *right.*

Perhaps there is only one way to really know the man you love.

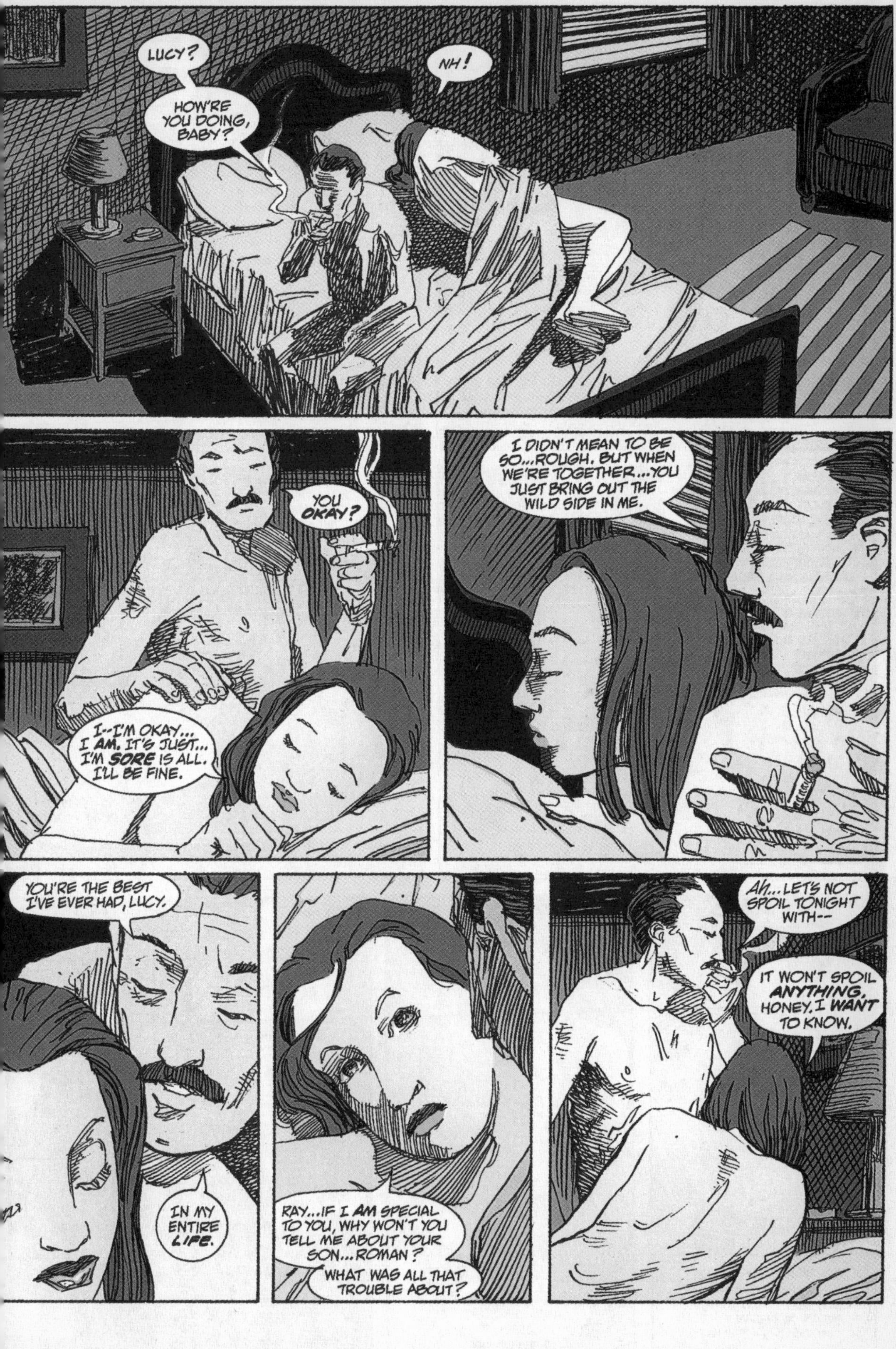
LUCY?
HOW'RE YOU DOING, BABY?
NH!
YOU OKAY?
I--I'M OKAY... I AM. IT'S JUST... I'M SORE IS ALL. I'LL BE FINE.
I DIDN'T MEAN TO BE SO...ROUGH. BUT WHEN WE'RE TOGETHER...YOU JUST BRING OUT THE WILD SIDE IN ME.
YOU'RE THE BEST I'VE EVER HAD, LUCY.
IN MY ENTIRE LIFE.
RAY...IF I AM SPECIAL TO YOU, WHY WON'T YOU TELL ME ABOUT YOUR SON...ROMAN?
WHAT WAS ALL THAT TROUBLE ABOUT?
Ah...LET'S NOT SPOIL TONIGHT WITH--
IT WON'T SPOIL ANYTHING, HONEY. I WANT TO KNOW.

I FEEL SO *CLOSE* TO YOU, RAY. CLOSER THAN I EVER HAVE TO *ANYONE.* PLEASE... NO SECRETS.

RAY?

ROMAN'S A...*TROUBLED* BOY. I USED TO THINK IT WAS JUST BECAUSE OF WHAT HAPPENED BETWEEN HIS MOTHER AND ME BEFORE SHE DIED, BUT--

--THE TRUTH IS THAT WE *NEVER* REALLY GOT ALONG TOO WELL. HE'S BEEN A DISAPPOINTMENT SINCE DAY ONE.

LAST YEAR I JUST GAVE UP HOPE THAT HE'D *EVER* HAVE A LIFE OF HIS OWN. HE DROPPED OUT OF MEDICAL SCHOOL AND MOVED IN TO AN APARTMENT IN THE TENEMENTS DOWN IN GREENWICH VILLAGE.

SOMEWHERE HE GOT IT INTO HIS HEAD THAT HE COULD MAKE A LIVING AS AN *ARTIST.* PFAHH! IDIOT...

WELL, *I* THINK IT SOUNDS... ROMANTIC.

ROMANCE IS EXACTLY THE WORD I WAS THINKING OF *TOO*--

OH, RAY, I DON'T THINK I CAN--

DON'T WORRY, HONEY. I KNOW YOU'RE WORN OUT, BUT THAT DOESN'T MEAN YOU CAN'T HELP ME *ANOTHER* WAY.

NO, RAY, PLEASE... CAN'T WE JUST TALK--?

LET *ME* DO THE TALKING...

...LUCY, OH BABY...OH.... YEAH...

GRANT'S GY

'NIGHT, TED. SEE YOU TOMORROW.

TAP TOK TAP TOK

SSSHKK

WHAZZAT? WHO BACK DERE?

OH MUH GOODNESS! SWEET JESUS! WHATCHU--

SLEEP NOW, LOUIS MONROE.

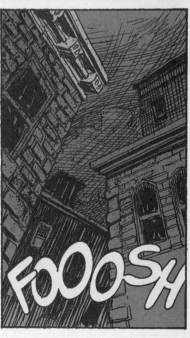

FOOOSH

3

DR. DEATH
act three

SLUNK

HEAR ME, LOUIS MONROE...

DAMN... TOO MUCH GAS.

4

HEAR ME, LOUIS MONROE...

HUH?...THAT YOU, TED? I'M OKAY... LET ME KEEP ON FIGHTIN'...I'LL GET UP IN A MINNIT--

UNNNH!

YOU ARE NO LONGER AT THE GYM, BUT CAST YOUR MIND TO THE MEN YOU KNEW THERE.

YOUR *FRIEND*, EDDIE THE ENGINE, MADE DELIVERIES FOR SOMEONE. YOU WILL TELL ME *WHO*.

MONTRASELLI...I WARNED EDDIE, TED...I TOLD 'IM MONTRASELLI WEREN'T UP TA NO GOOD...NOW EDDIE'S...

...TED?...DON'T FEEL SO GOOD...THINK I MAY HAVE TO...TO...

THEN *SLEEP* NOW, LOUIS.

THERE WILL BE MORE DAYS OF FIGHTING FOR YOU IN THIS CITY--

--*MANY MORE DAYS!*

5

57

Here you are, Dian--

--A young, modern, independent woman--

Living in the largest, most exciting city in the world.

--And what are you doing?

Watching the sun come up... alone--

--Wondering where in that city your man-- well...some man is--

--And feeling-- just feeling--

--Lost.

But it ends today.

I refuse to let you wallow in this vapid, self-pity any longer.

There's only one way you're going to get through this, and that's proving what you know in your heart to be true.

And that's just what I intend to do, Wesley.

Do you hear me?

I've waited for you long enough.

6

HMM---
---NOT LIKE ROBERT TO BE--

LATE? *PERISH* THE THOUGHT. YOU MUST HAVE SET YOUR WATCH TO THE BANK ON THE CORNER WHICH *IS* NOTORIOUSLY FAST.

WHEREAS *I* ALWAYS ALIGN TO GREENWICH MEAN.

I WAS STARTING TO THINK THAT YOU HAD FAILED IN YOUR CHALLENGE, SOCIETY BROTHER.

FAILED? HA!

A LIST OF THE 134 PRACTICING, LEFT-HANDED PHYSICIANS IN MANHATTAN--

--PLUS AN ADDENDUM OF THE 22 AMBIDEXTRIANS.

I AM IMPRESSED...

TWO EGGS, POACHED, TOAST, DRY, AND COFFEE. WES?

HMM? OH...NO NOTHING FOR ME, THANKS.

WELL? HAVE YOU FORGOTTEN *YOUR* TASK? TWO PAGES OF THE *TIMES*? MEMORIZED? UNLESS, OF COURSE, YOU'VE FAILED.

FAILED? HEH--

"POPEYE! YOU TOOK SWEETPEA ON THE SEA HAG'S SHIP AND THEN FORGOT HIM?!--"

SAAAY...WHAT *IS* THIS?

TWO PAGES FROM THE *TIMES*...TWO *FUNNY* PAGES, THAT IS--

"ARF! ARF! ARF! NOW LOOKS HERE, OLIVE--"

SNEAKY... BUT SHREWD!

7

There's no point in trying to sneak your way past me either, Wesley.

No "early morning meetings" or "want-everything-to-be perfects" will save you tonight.

BLOOMINGD...

I'm ready for you.

All of you...

...Inside...

...And out.

ABSOLUTELY, WANDA. BE AS DARING AS YOU LIKE.

SPECIAL NIGHT TONIGHT?

THE MOST SPECIAL.

No distractions.

I want you lost in my eyes, my scent, my body--

I want you lost in me.

8

IF THERE'S ANYTHING IN THE WORLD BETTER THAN THE TASTE OF THIS MATZO BALL SOUP, I *SURE* DON'T KNOW WHAT IT IS.

SLURP!

MMMM! MMMM!

YEAH, THE *REUBEN* HERE IS GOOD *TOO*. THANKS FOR BRINGIN' ME TO LUNCH.

MY PLEASURE, RALPH. HELPS TO CLEAR OUR MINDS IF WE GET OUT OF THE LAB.

AND I'LL *TELL* YOU, I'M *MORE* THAN A LITTLE CONFUSED ABOUT THESE TWO KILLINGS.

WE KNOW THAT THE ALCOHOL IS REACTING WITH SOME BASE COMPOUND IN THE BODY, BUT HOW? HOW IS THE BASE INTRODUCED? THERE *HAS* TO BE A COMMON--

WAIT A MINUTE. WAIT *JUST* A MINUTE.

...SMUDGED...

SCRUFFLE

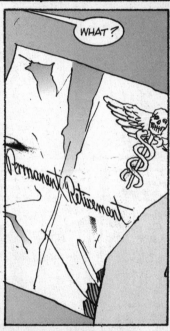

WHAT?

Permanent Retirement

RALPH, HAVE YOU TOUCHED EITHER NOTICE SINCE THIS ALL STARTED? HANDLED THEM IN *ANY* WAY?

NO, I DON'T *THINK* SO, WHY?

IF WHAT I SUSPECT IS *TRUE*, THESE PRESCRIPTIONS COULD BE FATAL--

OH DEAR...

RALPH! I HAVE TO GET OVER TO THE TIMES BEFORE THE EVENING EDITION GETS SET. I'LL MEET YOU BACK AT THE OFFICE LATER!

9

CALL FOR YOU, MISTER DODDS. ADAM CANTER OF THE W.P.A.

COULD YOU TELL HIM I'LL CALL BACK IN A *BIT*, JOYCE? I'M RIGHT IN THE MIDDLE OF SOMETHING.

CERTAINLY.

TURNER? TURNER... HMM...

Thompson, Eleaine
Thompson, George
Tolles, Michael
Tonik, Lawrence
Turner, B.S.
Turner, John
Turrentino, Jos
Uban, Th

"...BLACK AND WHITE...ALWAYS BLACK AND WHITE..."

HELLO? I'M HOPING TO SCHEDULE AN APPOINT- MENT WITH DR. RAYMOND KESSLER?...OH HE'S NOT? HM?...

OH I *SEE*. WELL ACTUALLY, THIS IS A HOUSE CALL OF SORTS...AN OFFICE CALL REALLY...

...NO NO, TODAY WAS JUST WHAT I HAD IN *MIND*... 5:00 IT IS...422 MADISON... YES. THANK YOU VERY MUCH.

JOYCE.

YES, MR. DODDS?

I'LL BE SEEING A DR. KESSLER AT 5:00 TODAY, AND I'D LIKE *NOT* TO BE DISTURBED UNTIL THEN.

YES, MR. DODDS.

10

MR. DODDS? DR. KESSLER IS HERE TO SEE YOU NOW.

THANK YOU. SHOW HIM RIGHT IN.

TAP TAP TAP

TAP... TAP...

RAYMOND, A PLEASURE TO SEE YOU AGAIN!

REALLY? I'D HAVE THOUGHT A MEDICAL MALADY WOULDN'T TECHNICALLY *QUALIFY* AS A "PLEASURE," BUT SUIT YOURSELF.

SPEAKING OF THE SAME, MY SECRETARY FORGOT TO ASK YOU WHAT YOUR PROBLEM SPECIFICALLY *IS...?*

HEADACHES MOSTLY, AND A HORRIBLE BOUT OF INSOMNIA.

Mm hm. WHY DON'T YOU GO AHEAD AND LOOSEN YOUR SHIRT?

ARE THESE *NEW* SYMPTOMS OR PERSISTENT?

I'D SAY THE HEADACHES ARE RECENT, BUT THE INSOMNIA IS BORDER-ING ON *CHRONIC.*

YOU'RE SAYING YOU DON'T SLEEP?

NOT *WELL.*

THAT'S A TOUGH NUT, I KNOW.

11

63

I *USED* TO BE LIKE THAT MYSELF, WHEN I WAS CRAWLING UP THROUGH THE RANKS. BUT *THESE* NIGHTS, I'M OUT LIKE A CANDLE.

I SEEM TO WAKE EVERY NIGHT IN A START.

SOUNDS TO ME LIKE THE PRESSURES OF THE WORKPLACE MIGHT BE GETTING THE BETTER OF YOU.

POSSIBLY.

STRANGE...

...YOUR BLOOD PRESSURE'S LOWER THAN *MINE.* I'D HAVE EXPECTED IT TO BE *HIGHER* IF YOU WERE OVERWORKED.

YOU KNOW, I SAW YOUR FRIEND'S NAME IN THE PAPER YESTERDAY... DR. TURNER?

TAKE A DEEP BREATH--

--TURNER, EH? HE DIDN'T *MENTION* IT TO ME. MEETING HIM FOR DRINKS TONIGHT. I'LL HAVE TO ASK HIM ABOUT IT--

--AND *EXHALE.*

YOU KNOW, MAYBE IT WAS JUST A *SIMILAR* NAME. STILL, HE CAME TO MIND.

NICE FELLOW.

SURE. HE'S ALMOST WHITE.

LISTEN, I'M GOING TO GIVE YOU A PRESCRIPTION FOR SOME SEDATIVES, BUT MY PERSONAL OPINION IS THAT WHAT YOU REALLY NEED IS SOME TIME OFF.

YOU'RE AN UPTIGHT SORT, DODDS. A LITTLE *FUN* WOULD DO YOU MORE GOOD THAN AN ENTIRE *BOTTLE* OF PILLS.

DODDS?

SORRY, I WAS JUST ADMIRING YOUR PEN.

YOU SEE WHAT I MEAN? COME ON, DODDS. *RELAX!* WHY DON'T YOU JOIN TURNER AND ME AT THE REPUBLIC TONIGHT?

YOU KNOW, I THINK MAYBE YOU'RE RIGHT. I'LL *DO* IT.

GOOD MAN! BRAVO!

1

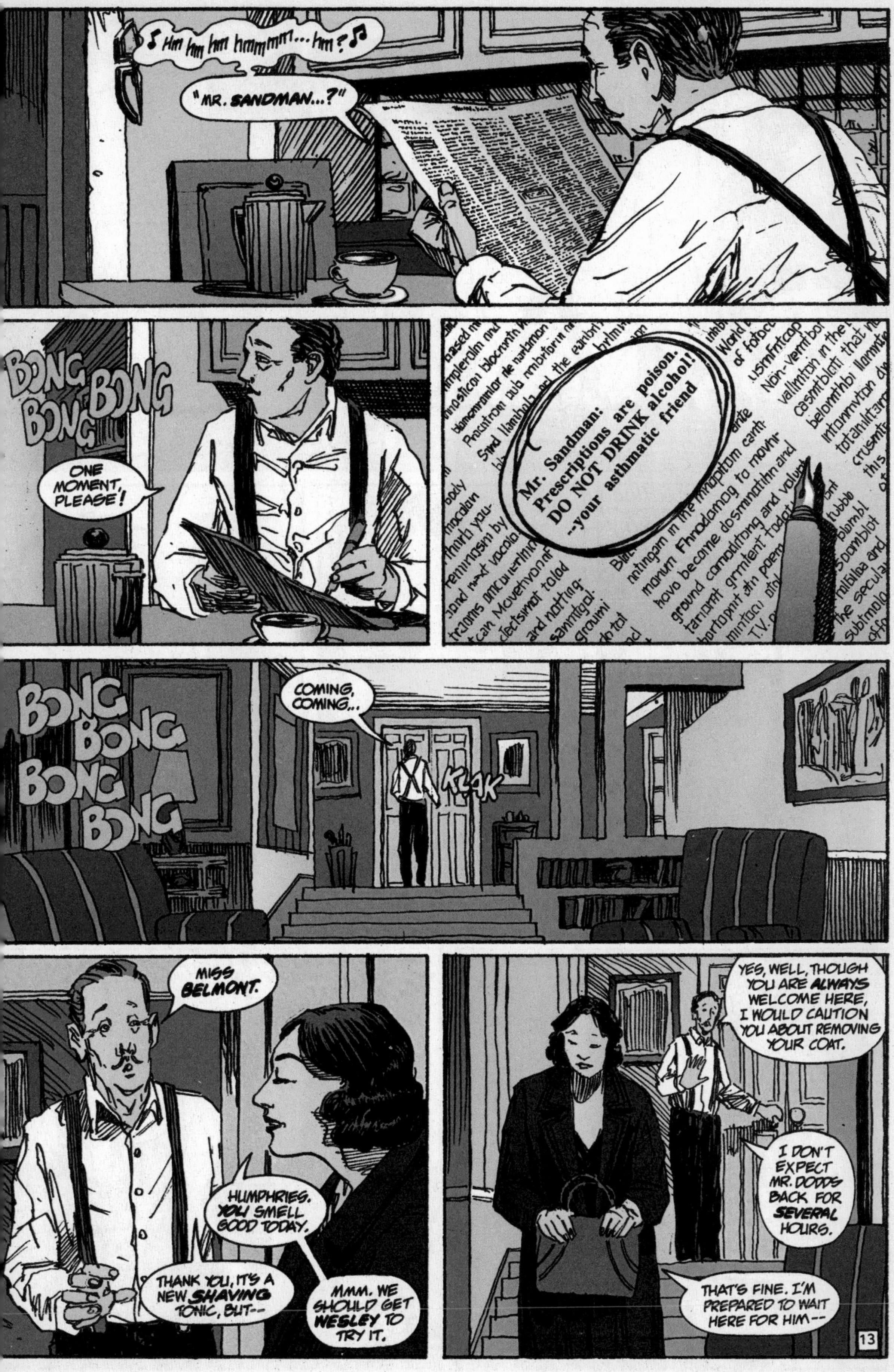
Hm hm hm hmmmm... hm?
"MR. SANDMAN...?"
BONG BONG BONG BONG
ONE MOMENT, PLEASE!
Mr. Sandman: Prescriptions are poison. DO NOT DRINK alcohol! --your asthmatic friend
BONG BONG BONG BONG
COMING, COMING...
KLAK
MISS BELMONT.
HUMPHRIES. YOU SMELL GOOD TODAY.
THANK YOU, IT'S A NEW SHAVING TONIC, BUT--
MMM. WE SHOULD GET WESLEY TO TRY IT.
YES, WELL, THOUGH YOU ARE ALWAYS WELCOME HERE, I WOULD CAUTION YOU ABOUT REMOVING YOUR COAT.
I DON'T EXPECT MR. DODDS BACK FOR SEVERAL HOURS.
THAT'S FINE. I'M PREPARED TO WAIT HERE FOR HIM--
13

...ALL NIGHT... IF I HAVE TO.

I... SEE. CAN I-- CAN I HELP YOU WITH YOUR *BAG?*

NO THANK YOU. I'LL TAKE IT UP-STAIRS MYSELF *LATER.*

I'M SORRY I DIDN'T CALL EARLIER TO *ALERT* YOU, HUMPHRIES, BUT THIS IS SORT OF A *SURPRISE* FOR WES.

I'M SURE IT *WILL* BE, YES. CAN I HELP YOU WITH YOUR--YOUR--

MY COAT? THANK YOU.

HUMPHRIES? COULD YOU BE A DEAR AND ENTER-TAIN YOURSELF... *OUT* TONIGHT?

OUT?

YES. YOU SEE, WESLEY AND I HAVE SOME *MATTERS* TO RESOLVE TONIGHT. SOME VERY *PRIVATE* MATTERS.

I'M SORRY, BUT MASTER DODDS EXPECTS ME TO--

HUMPHRIES, I'M *CERTAIN* THAT MR. DODDS WOULD APPRECIATE YOUR UNDER-STANDING IN THIS AS MUCH AS *I* WOULD...

I'LL BE *MORE* THAN HAPPY TO TAKE CARE OF ANYTHING WES MAY NEED--

--AND I'M SURE WE *BOTH* WOULD APPRECIATE COMPLETE PRIVACY TONIGHT.

YES... I IMAGINE.

14

BUT I MUST TELL--

YOU'RE NOT GOING TO MAKE ME *FIGHT* WITH YOU ABOUT THIS... *ARE* YOU?

NO... I SUPPOSE NOT. BUT IN RETURN, I MUST ASK A FAVOR OF YOU. A *CONFIDENTIAL* FAVOR.

OF COURSE.

I SEE THAT YOU'VE BROUGHT WITH YOU A BOTTLE OF *SPIRITS* FOR THIS EVENING'S... FESTIVITIES.

BEING THE *PERCEPTIVE* WOMAN THAT YOU CLEARLY ARE, I TRUST YOU'VE NOTICED MR. DODDS' AVERSION TO DRINK?

WELL, I HAVE, BUT I THOUGHT I MIGHT CONVINCE HIM JUST THIS ONCE--

ABSOLUTELY NOT. THOUGH HE IS USUALLY TOO ASHAMED TO ADMIT IT, MR. DODDS IS *DEATHLY* ALLERGIC TO ALCOHOL OF ANY *SORT.*

REALLY? BUT HE'S NEVER SAID A THING ABOUT IT.

WELL, IT'S NOT THE SORT OF THING A MAN TAKES PRIDE IN ADMITTING. WHY, TO EVEN *OFFER* COULD SPOIL YOUR ENTIRE EVENING.

THANK YOU, HUMPHRIES. CONSIDER IT TAKEN CARE OF.

MARVELOUS. GOOD EVENING TO YOU BOTH THEN, MISS.

GOOD NIGHT.

Another secret.

15

Where does it all end?

WOOOOOO!

--LET US SEE IT!

--I'M DYIN' OVUH HEAH--

GENTLEMEN! STEP RIGHT IN! BEAUTIES, BEAUTIES, *BEAUTIES!*

BURLESC

BURLESQUE REPUBLIC

LYRIC   LYRIC

THAT'LL SURE RAISE YOUR MIZZENMAST, EH, FELLAS?

UH...

HOMINA--

WHY, DR. TURNER, I DO BELIEVE OUR NEW FRIEND IS *BLUSHING.*

HE'S STILL *LOOKING,* ISN'T HE?

HA HA HA!

HEY, SPORTS, DRINKS?

DEFINITELY. MARTINI, DRY.

AND I'LL--

UH, JUST A SELTZER, PLEASE!

BACK IN A MINUTE!

HEY!

JEEZ, MISTER! WHAT'RE YA *DOIN'?*

YOU DIDN'T GET MY *OTHER* FRIEND'S ORDER.

LOOK, WE LET 'EM *IN,* BUT WE DON'T *SERVE* 'EM.

YOU'LL BRING HIM A BOURBON OR YOU'LL ANSWER TO *ME.* UNDERSTAND?

ALL RIGHT ALREADY. SHEESH!

16

GENTLEMEN, THE WINGED WOMAN OF PARIS, FRANCE... GENEVIEVE!

CLAP CLAP CLAP CLAP

WELL THAT WAS REALLY SOMETHING.

THAT WAS *MORE* THAN SOMETHING, WES, THAT WAS *TWO* SOMETHINGS.

YOU'LL HAVE TO PARDON RAY, HE *DOES* LOVE THE LADIES.

I TAKE IT THIS ISN'T YOUR USUAL HAUNT, WESLEY?

NO, I'VE ALWAYS BEEN A LITTLE UNCOMFORTABLE LOVING THE LADIES THAT I DON'T *KNOW*.

YOU KNOW 'EM BETTER AFTER YOU'VE SEEN 'EM *HERE*.

BESIDES, I'D'VE NEVER MET LUCY IF I *WASN'T* A CUSTOMER HERE.

REALLY? *LUCY* WAS A DANCER HERE? I'D NEVER HAVE --

DANCER? HELL *NO!* I'D NEVER BED DOWN WITH A *WHORE!* NAH. I MET A GUY HERE WHO SUGGESTED LUCY'S DAD'S STABLES FOR MY HORSE.

OH...I'M SORRY. I DIDN'T MEAN TO SUGGEST--

NO HARM DONE. LIGHTEN UP, WES. DOCTOR'S ORDERS.

NOW IF YOU GENTS'LL EXCUSE ME, I GOTTA HIT THE BACK ROOM FOR A LEAK.

OR *SOMETHING*.

WATCH THE LIP OR I WON'T GET YOU ANY MORE DRINKS!

NOT *THAT!*

17

SO...RAYMOND TELLS ME YOU'VE STOPPED PERFORMING SURGERY?

Hmm? OH...SURE, NOTHING SERIOUS, I JUST THOUGHT I'D BE... HAPPIER IN ADMINISTRATION. MORE MONEY...YOU KNOW.

DON'T YOU MISS THE--

WILL YOU LOOK AT THAT! HERE'S ANOTHER YOUNG LADY!

VERY YOUNG, DON'T YOU THINK?

I'VE GOT NO PROBLEM WITH THAT--

WHO WANTS 'EM WHEN THEY'RE SAGGY AND FAT?

COME NOW, NOT ALL OLDER WOMEN ARE--

WHOOOO BABY!

HERE'S YOUR DRINKS.

THANK YOU VERY MUCH.

DON'T THANK ME TOO MUCH. AIN'T LIKE THEY'RE A CHRISTMAS PRESENT. SOMEBODY'S GOTTA PAY FOR--

WE'LL RUN A TAB.

BUT--

IT'S OKAY. I'LL SIGN FOR IT!

18

70

--WUZZA GOOD START! NOW LET'S HEAD OVER TO TH' *IRISH* FOR SOME WHISKEY.

I APPRECIATE THE INVITE, BUT I'M AFRAID I'M BUSHED. I'D BETTER CALL IT A NIGHT.

ALREADY? C'MON!

DODDS...YOU ARE... *INCURABLE.*

SORRY, BUT I WAS UP AT FIVE THIS MORNING AND--

WESLEY'S RIGHT, RAY. IT *IS* LATE AND I PROMISED MY WIFE I'D BE BACK EARLY. MIND IF I SHARE YOUR CAB, WES?

AWW, NOT YOU *TOO,* TURNER.

OH... UH...WELL...SURE...

WHAT KINDA SAPS DID I HOOK UP WITH?

APPARENTLY, THE *TIRED* KIND, RAYMOND. GOOD NIGHT AND THANKS.

YOU TWO MUST BE *DEAD.* HOW CAN YOU GET ALL ROUSED UP AND JUST--AW, NEVER MIND, SEE YOO 'ROUND.

BOB! BOB!

HUH? WHAT IS IT, CANDY? FIGHT?

NO, WORSE.

IT'S RITA-- SHE'S REALLY SICK.

THROWIN' UP ALL OV--

IT'S ALWAYS SOMETHIN' WIDDAT OLD HAG.

GET OUTTA TH' WAY!

19

HUMPHRIES?

CHANGE IN PLANS--

KLAK

--TURNER JUMPED MY LAB, SO I'M HEADING RIGHT BACK OUT TO--

SWIK

--HUMPHRIES...?

♪♪♪

HM.

♪♪♪

...HUMPHRIES?

BUT THAT'S MY...

♪♪♪

...PHONOGRAPH.

♪♪♪

WHAT--?

♪♪♪

THERE YOU ARE, MYSTERY MAN. COME IN--

20

--I'VE BEEN WAITING FOR YOU.

DIAN? I--I DIDN'T EXPECT-- YOU'RE--

--MY GOD, DIAN...

WHAT'S THE MATTER? DON'T YOU *LIKE* HOW I LOOK TONIGHT? I BOUGHT IT JUST FOR *YOU.*

WHAT *IS* IT, WES?

WHAT'S *STOPPING* US?

ONLY OURSELVES.

LET'S *NOT* STOP TONIGHT.

DIAN? HAVE YOU BEEN *DRINKING?*

JUST A LITTLE *WINE.* I WAS *NERVOUS.*

HM. MAYBE I SHOULD *JOIN* YOU...

NO!

I MEAN... LET *ME* RELAX YOU.

LET ME BE YOUR NECTAR TONIGHT.

MMMMMM

WE *HAVE* ALL NIGHT, MY LOVE...

21

DIAN... ARE YOU *SURE*?

VERY.

NOW STOP TALKING. LET'S *REALLY* LEARN ABOUT EACH OTHER...

OH...

mmmm...

UNH-UNH-UNH--

HNNNH! NNH

OH... WES... LEY...

22

Oh Wesley...

...This is what nights are for.

Not secrets --

--Or sneaking--

-- Or violence.

Is *that* what's kept us apart? Were you afraid what I would think of the scars you carry?

Were you afraid of what I might ask?

There is no place for fear between us --

--Just as there is no longer any place for deception.

23

I'm sorry it had to be like this, Wesley...

TUNK

THE INTERPRE of DREAM S. FREUD

CLACK

...But I have to know.

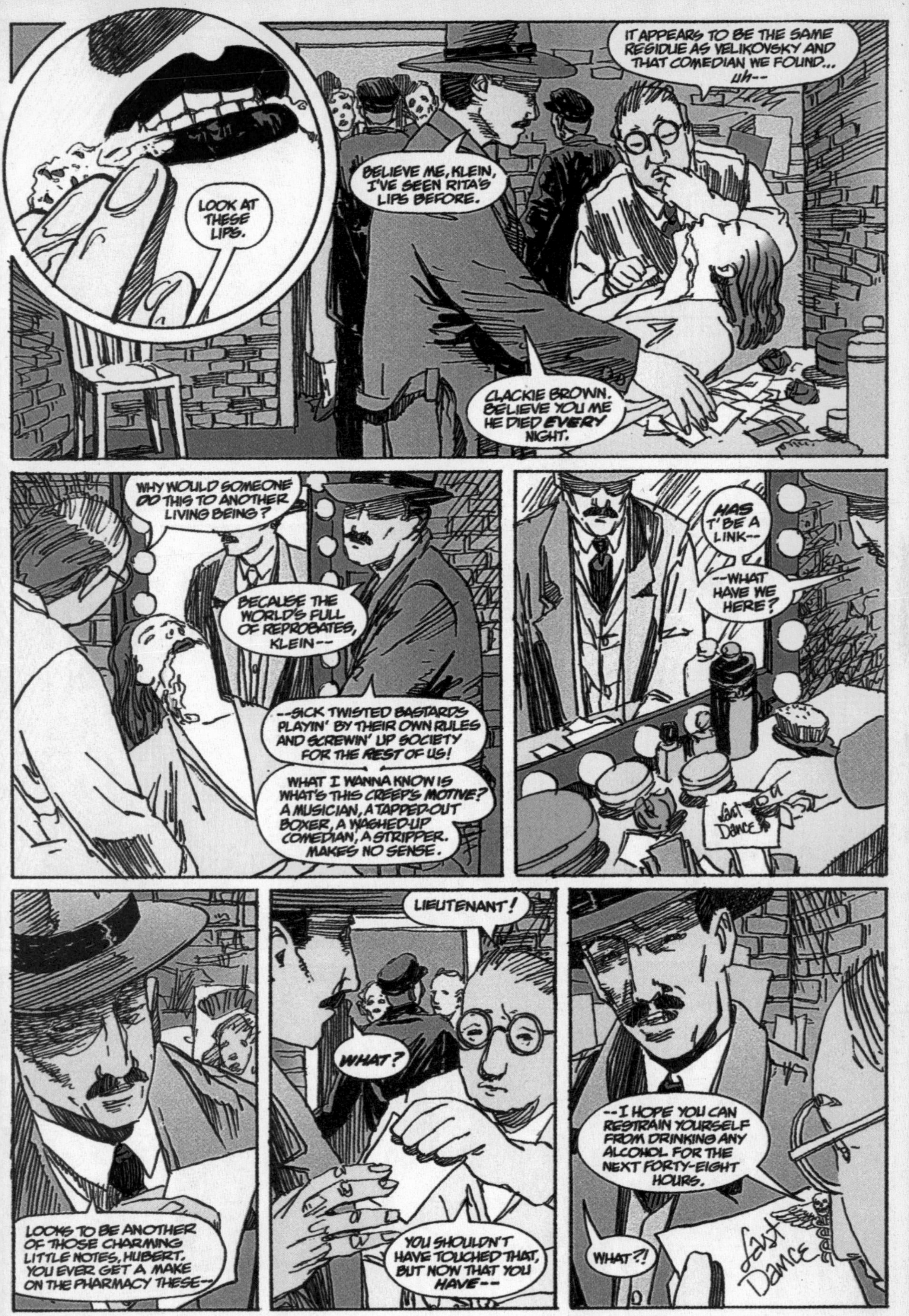
LOOK AT THESE LIPS.
BELIEVE ME, KLEIN, I'VE SEEN RITA'S LIPS BEFORE.
IT APPEARS TO BE THE SAME RESIDUE AS VELIKOVSKY AND THAT COMEDIAN WE FOUND... uh--
CLACKIE BROWN. BELIEVE YOU ME HE DIED EVERY NIGHT.
WHY WOULD SOMEONE DO THIS TO ANOTHER LIVING BEING?
BECAUSE THE WORLD'S FULL OF REPROBATES, KLEIN--
--SICK TWISTED BASTARDS PLAYIN' BY THEIR OWN RULES AND SCREWIN' UP SOCIETY FOR THE REST OF US!
WHAT I WANNA KNOW IS WHAT'S THIS CREEP'S MOTIVE? A MUSICIAN, A TAPPED-OUT BOXER, A WASHED-UP COMEDIAN, A STRIPPER. MAKES NO SENSE.
HAS T'BE A LINK--
--WHAT HAVE WE HERE?
Last Dance
LOOKS TO BE ANOTHER OF THOSE CHARMING LITTLE NOTES, HUBERT. YOU EVER GET A MAKE ON THE PHARMACY THESE--
LIEUTENANT!
WHAT?
YOU SHOULDN'T HAVE TOUCHED THAT, BUT NOW THAT YOU HAVE--
--I HOPE YOU CAN RESTRAIN YOURSELF FROM DRINKING ANY ALCOHOL FOR THE NEXT FORTY-EIGHT HOURS.
WHAT?!
Last Dance

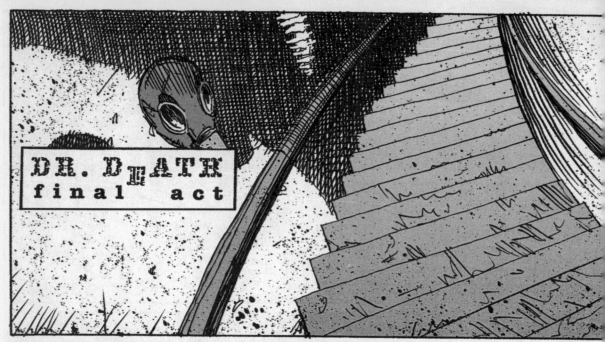

DR. DEATH
final act

I wish I could stop walking.

CREEEK

OH GOD...
WESLEY...

I know what lies at the end of this corridor. Two outcomes, neither of them pleasant.

I confirm my suspicions and shatter my relationship with Wesley--

--or I fail to confirm them and destroy any trust we've built between us.

OH!

...IT IS YOU.

I'VE BEEN TRYING TO FIND A WAY TO TELL YOU JUST THAT, DIAN--

WHA--?

--BUT NOW YOU'VE GONE AND CRACKED THE CASE ON YOUR OWN.

3

HEY! WHAT ARE *YOU* DOING HERE?

ROMAN? YOU STARTLED ME--

HOW DID YOU GET A KEY? I *BET* HE DIDN'T GIVE YOU ONE.

WHA--? WELL, I SAW THAT RAY,...UH, YOUR FATHER, KEPT ONE HIDDEN OUTSIDE.

CLIK

AND I--I WAS JUST BACK FROM A VISIT WITH MY PARENTS, IN THE COUNTRY, YOU KNOW, AND I THOUGHT I'D *SURPRISE* HIM.

A LITTLE LATE FOR SURPRISES--

--ISN'T IT?

KLATCH

WELL, I SUPPOSE THAT ALL DEPENDS ON WHAT *TYPE* OF SURPRISE YOU'RE SPEAKING ABOUT.

LISTEN, LUCKY, OR WHATEVER YOUR NAME IS, I'M *NOT* GONNA STAND HERE AND PLAY *GAMES* WITH YOU!

ANYWAY, YOU'RE WASTING YOUR TIME. RAYMOND'S NOT EVEN *HERE!*

NOT HERE? BUT--HE'S OUT? AT *THIS* HOUR?

WORD TO THE WISE--

--WHEN YOU'RE DEALING WITH KESSLER *SENIOR,* DON'T LEAVE HIM UNATTENDED FOR VERY LONG.

A STUD *TENDS* TO WANDER, YOU KNOW.

4

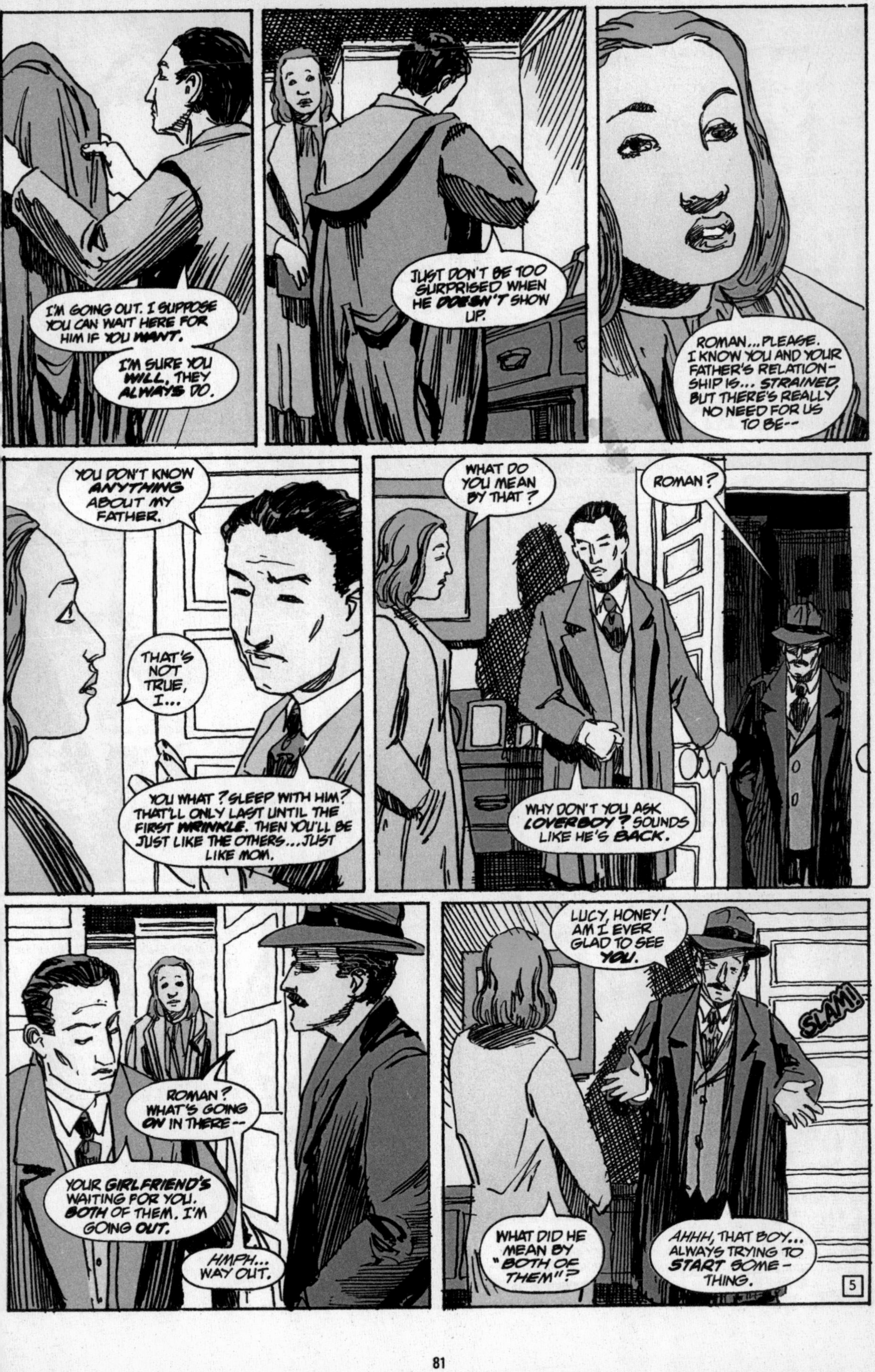
I'M GOING OUT. I SUPPOSE YOU CAN WAIT HERE FOR HIM IF YOU WANT.
I'M SURE YOU WILL, THEY ALWAYS DO.
JUST DON'T BE TOO SURPRISED WHEN HE DOESN'T SHOW UP.
ROMAN... PLEASE. I KNOW YOU AND YOUR FATHER'S RELATIONSHIP IS... STRAINED, BUT THERE'S REALLY NO NEED FOR US TO BE--
YOU DON'T KNOW ANYTHING ABOUT MY FATHER.
THAT'S NOT TRUE, I...
YOU WHAT? SLEEP WITH HIM? THAT'LL ONLY LAST UNTIL THE FIRST WRINKLE. THEN YOU'LL BE JUST LIKE THE OTHERS... JUST LIKE MOM.
WHAT DO YOU MEAN BY THAT?
ROMAN?
WHY DON'T YOU ASK LOVERBOY? SOUNDS LIKE HE'S BACK.
ROMAN? WHAT'S GOING ON IN THERE--
YOUR GIRLFRIEND'S WAITING FOR YOU. BOTH OF THEM. I'M GOING OUT.
HMPH... WAY OUT.
LUCY, HONEY! AM I EVER GLAD TO SEE YOU.
SLAM!
WHAT DID HE MEAN BY "BOTH OF THEM"?
AHHH, THAT BOY... ALWAYS TRYING TO START SOMETHING.
5

I ADMIRE YOUR SKILLS. REALLY.

CLICK

DON'T TRY TO SWEET TALK ME, MISTER.

I DON'T REALLY HAVE ANY EXCUSE FOR KEEPING ALL OF THIS COVERED UP, I JUST--

I KNOW THIS WAS VERY INTRUSIVE OF ME, BUT YOU WOULDN'T--

I'M SORRY, GO AHEAD.

NO, THAT'S ALL RIGHT. LADIES FIRST, PLEASE.

WESLEY, THESE PAST FEW MONTHS HAVE BEEN VERY SPECIAL FOR ME. I'VE HAD A NUMBER OF BOYS IN MY LIFE, BUT NEVER A MAN. NEVER SOMEONE I FELT I LOVED IN THE TRUE SENSE OF THE WORD. BUT I FELT THAT THERE WAS SOMETHING BETWEEN US.

NOW I SEE THAT MY SUSPICIONS WERE TRUE. THAT--

DIAN--

--THAT AFTER OUR FIRST NIGHT OF INTIMACY, YOU LEFT ME SLEEPING SO YOU COULD GO OUT AND CHASE HOODLUMS DRESSED LIKE--LIKE SOMETHING OUT OF A SILLY PULP MAGAZINE.

6

DIAN...YOU HAVE EVERY RIGHT TO BE ANGRY WITH ME, BUT SURELY YOU CAN SEE WHY I FOUND THIS A DIFFICULT SECRET TO TELL.

HELL, IN SOME WAYS I DON'T KNOW THAT I'VE FULLY ADMITTED THIS SIDE OF MY LIFE TO *MYSELF* YET.

WHEN I WALK THROUGH THAT PASSAGE, IT'S ALMOST AS IF I'M A DIFFERENT MAN. *SIMILAR,* BUT NOT ENTIRELY ME.

I'M NOT EVEN SURE HOW IT GOT *THIS* FAR. I NEVER *PICTURED* MYSELF TRYING TO RIGHT THE WORLD'S WRONGS, NOT EVEN A SMALL PORTION OF THEM.

BUT I HAVE THESE DREAMS...*CONSTANTLY.* VISIONS OF TERRIBLE, DEPRAVED PEOPLE.

YOU'RE SAYING YOU *DREAM* ABOUT THESE CRIMINALS AND FEEL COMPELLED TO PURSUE THEM?

WELL...YES, AND THE DREAMS ONLY SUBSIDE WHEN I'VE PUT A STOP TO THESE CREATURES.

AND THEN, JUST WHEN I HOPE IT'S ALL OVER, ANOTHER DREAM, ANOTHER VISION COMES AND I--

THIS IS TOO STRANGE...

PLEASE, DIAN, I KNOW HOW FARFETCHED IT SOUNDS, BUT IT'S TRUE. I SWEAR TO YOU IT'S--

FARFETCHED? IT'S FANTASTIC!

DIAN? PLEASE. LET'S TALK THIS OUT. I--I FEEL LIKE A GREAT BURDEN HAS BEEN--

DIAN?

PLEASE DON'T GO, I--

I'M SORRY, WESLEY. THIS HAS SUDDENLY GOTTEN A LITTLE TOO WEIRD FOR ME.

7

83

RAY! STOP IT. YOU'RE DRUNK, AND YOU--YOU SMELL ...FUNNY.

SMELL FU--

THA'S JUST THE SMELL OF LOVE, HONEY. SMELLIN' MY SPORE, DARLIN'.

C'MERE AN' HAVE A DRINK WITH RAY.

I AM WORRIED, RAY. I'VE NEVER SEEN YOU LIKE THIS. WHERE WERE YOU AT THIS HOUR OF THE NIGHT?

YOU JEALOUS? HUH? I WAS OUT WITH SOME FRIENDS. AN' THAT'S ALL.

RAY...YOU'VE GOT...THERE'S LIPSTICK ALL OVER YOUR SHIRT! AND NOW I KNOW WHAT THAT SMELL IS! IT'S CHEAP PERFUME! YOU'VE BEEN OUT WITH ANOTHER WOMAN!

HOW DARE YOU!

LUCY...YOU KNOW ME BETTER'N THAT.

YOU...YOU KNOW THAT NO MATTER WHAT ELSE I MAY DO---

--I'LL ALWAYS HAVE PLENTY A JUICE LEFT FOR MY FAVORITE FILLY.

SLAP!

THAT'S NOT HOW WE DO THIS, LITTLE GIRL. I'LL SHOW YOU WHAT THAT KINDA PLAY GETS YOU WITH A REAL MAN!

8

DIAN!

I SUPPOSE NEXT YOU'LL TELL ME YOU'VE SEEN A MAN FROM MARS.

DIAN, I *KNOW* THIS IS DIFFICULT, BUT PLEASE STAY. I FEEL--I FEEL VERY *CLOSE* TO YOU RIGHT NOW AND--

AND IS THIS HOW YOU *TREAT* THE PEOPLE YOU'RE CLOSE TO?

BY *LYING* TO THEM?. CLOUDING YOUR LIFE WITH MYSTERIES AND DELUSIONS SO THEY CAN'T REALLY *SEE* YOU? WHERE'S THE MORALITY IN *THAT*? WHERE'S THE *JUSTICE*?

THE *JUSTICE* IS THAT DESPITE HOW I'VE HURT YOU, AND I *KNOW I HAVE*, THAT I ALSO *HELP* PEOPLE. INNOCENT SOULS WHO HAVE NO ONE ELSE TO TURN TO.

HOW *MODEST* OF YOU TO DISMISS THE WORK OF SOME OF THE CITY'S FINEST MEN, NOT TO MENTION MY FATHER'S ENTIRE CAREER--

WHY, EVEN NOW, THERE'S A CRAZED DOCTOR WRITING AND FILLING PRESCRIPTIONS OF HATE, KILLING THE CITY'S OLDER FOLK.

THE POLICE HAVE *NO* LEADS, I KNOW. I WAS LISTENING TO THEIR--

SO *YOU'RE* OUT HUNTING FOR THIS--THIS "DOCTOR OF DEATH"?

THAT'S *EXACTLY* WHAT I DON'T LIKE ABOUT THIS WHOLE SITUATION, WES.

JUST LISTEN TO YOURSELF. DOCTORS DON'T *HURT* PEOPLE. THIS IS LIKE A BAD DREA--

DIAN--

--OHHH...

9

85

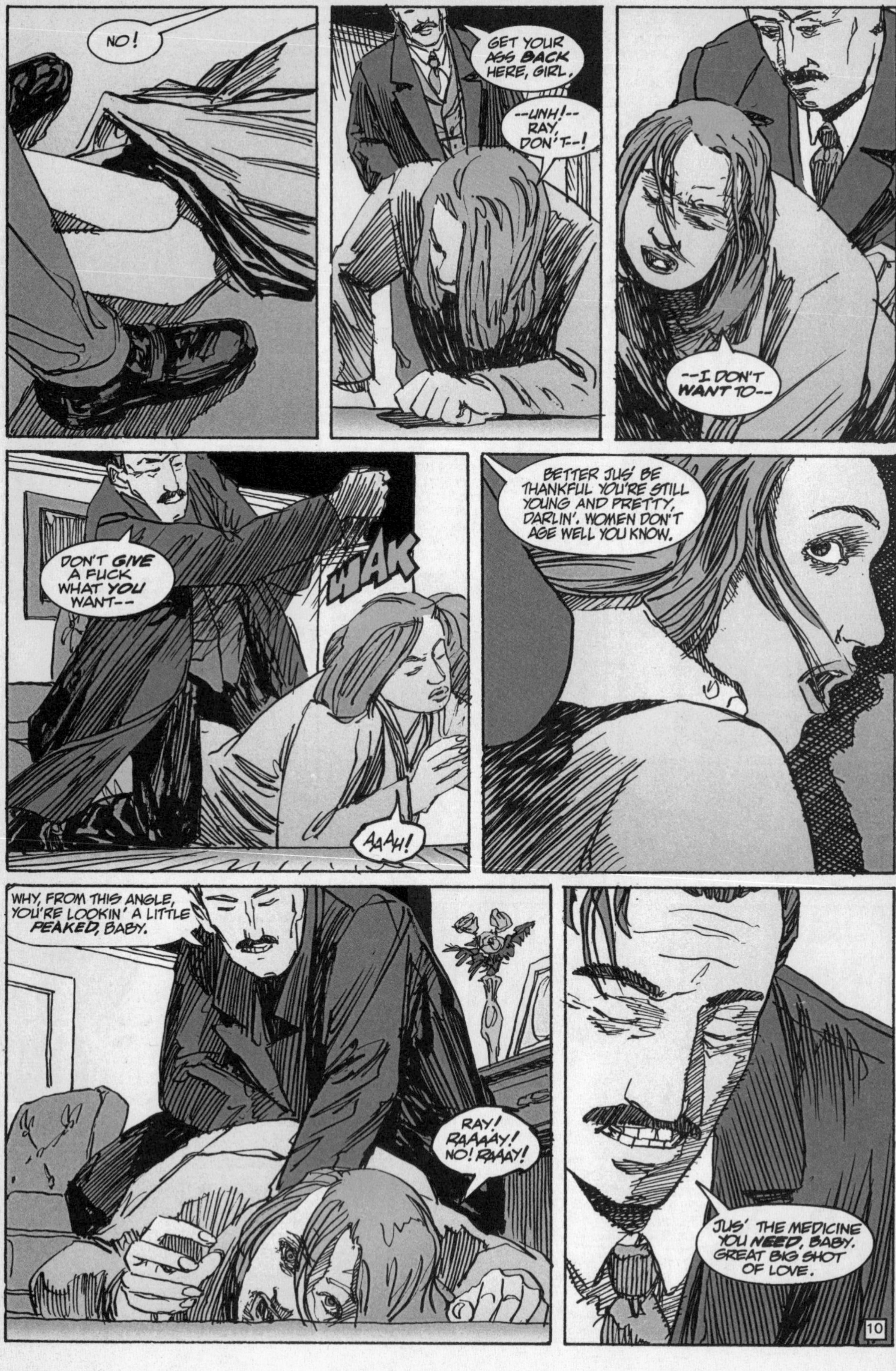
NO!
GET YOUR ASS BACK HERE, GIRL.
--UNH!-- RAY, DON'T--!
--I DON'T WANT TO--
DON'T GIVE A FUCK WHAT YOU WANT--
WAK
AAAH!
BETTER JUS' BE THANKFUL YOU'RE STILL YOUNG AND PRETTY, DARLIN'. WOMEN DON'T AGE WELL YOU KNOW.
WHY, FROM THIS ANGLE, YOU'RE LOOKIN' A LITTLE PEAKED, BABY.
RAY! RAAAAY! NO! RAAAY!
JUS' THE MEDICINE YOU NEED, BABY. GREAT BIG SHOT OF LOVE.
10

DON'T GO. I KNOW HOW STRANGE THIS MUST SEEM TO YOU, *HONESTLY*, BUT DON'T LET THIS PUT A WALL BETWEEN US.

I--I HAVE TO--

IF ONLY YOU WOULD TRY TO *UNDERSTAND*. THIS ISN'T A FANTASY, DIAN.

IT'S *REAL*. YOU HAVE TO BELIEVE ME. STAY. TALK TO ME.

I'M SORRY, WES, BUT I NEED SOME TIME TO *THINK* ABOUT THIS.

I DON'T KNOW IF I CAN TRUST YOU ANYMORE. AND I DON'T KNOW IF WHAT I FEEL ABOUT YOU IS *SAFE*.

DIAN, I'M NOT TELLING YOU SOME TALL TALE--

--THIS IS *REAL*--

IT'S... IT'S...

SHIT.

11

TOO MUCH WHISKEY TONIGHT, DR. TURNER...

... WHY YOU LET KESSLER TALK YOU INTO IT?

...KESSLER...

AH, DON'T LIE TO YOURSELF--

--ONLY MAKE YOUR STOMACH WORSE--

FLITCH

TURNER.

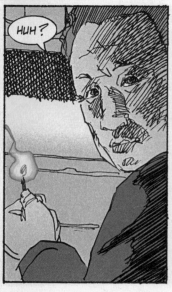

HUH?

WARM MILK MAY TAKE YOU TO THE LAND OF DREAMS IN TIME--

OH!

--BUT I WOULD SEE YOU THERE MUCH SOONER.

FOOSH!

12

HEAR ME, JOHN TURNER--

--YOU SWORE AN OATH TO HIPPOCRATES WHICH YOU HAVE TAKEN IN VAIN FOR TOO LONG. YOUR TIME OF ATONEMENT IS *UPON* YOU!

CONFESS.

BUROR--UNH...YES... I...I PADDED OUT BUDGETS--LAST TWO YEARS AT HOSPITAL--

-- HOOTCHIED THAT NURSE IN EMERGENCY FOUR TIMES NOW... CHEATED ON MEDICAL BOARDS... GOT ANSWERS FROM--

THESE *ARE* SORDID TRANSGRESSIONS. BUT WHAT OF YOUR *DEADLY* PRESCRIPTIONS?

PRE-PRESCRIPTIONS...? HAVEN'T WRITTEN ANY SINCE I QUIT MY PRACTICE...YEARS AGO...

DAMN IT! I'VE WASTED MY TIME ON YOU AND DR. KESSLER.

KESSLER? HE'S NO... NOT DOCTOR... NOT--

WHAT DO YOU MEAN?

NOT A DOCTOR...KNOWN HIM FOR YEARS...MOVED FUNNY MONEY AND SMACK--CHICAGO... THEN MOVED HERE... SIX, EIGHT YEARS AN' SUDDENLY HE'S A *DOCTOR*...?

...GIMME A BREAK...

KLAK KLAK

JOHN? ARE YOU IN--

JOHN? WHAT IS IT? *TELL* ME!

...STILL LOVE YOU, HONEY... JUST NOT *ATTRACTED* TO YOU ANYMORE...

WHAT!?

13

89

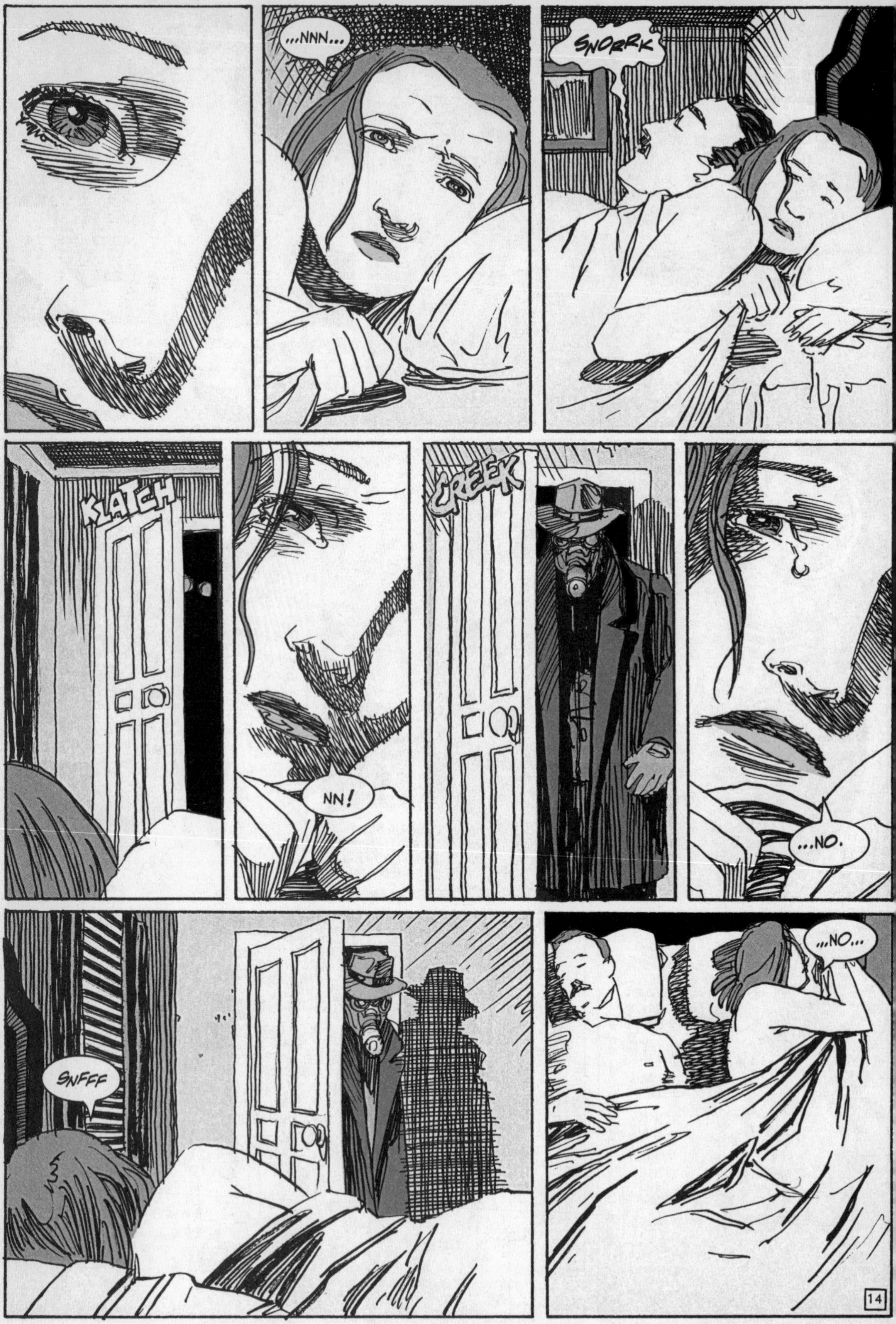
...NNN...
SNORRK
KLATCH
NN!
CREEK
...NO.
SNFFF
...NO...
14

DAMN IT.

YAAWWWN.

HUBERT KLEIN?. THE SANDMAN HAS NEED OF YOUR KNOWLEDGE.

THANK GOODNESS YOU'VE CALLED. DID YOU GET MY MESSAGE?

MESSAGE?

IN THE TIMES. IT WAS LATE BUT I HAVE A FRIEND THERE WHO GOT IT IN. ABOUT NOT DRINKING ALCOHOL?

THE PRESCRIPTION CARDS CONTAIN A STRANGE CHEMICAL BASE COMPOUND-- INCREDIBLY STRONG. I'VE NEVER SEEN ANYTHING LIKE IT. THE ACIDS IN ALCOHOL ARE THE CATALYST. IF YOU'VE TOUCHED ONE OF THOSE CARDS BARE-HANDED, YOU MUST STAY AWAY FROM ANY LIQUOR.

I DON'T... HAVEN'T HANDLED IT UNGLOVED. I NEED YOU TO CHECK A MEDICAL LICENSE FOR ME.

A SUSPECT?

A PRACTITIONER I HAVE REASON TO BELIEVE IS NOT A DOCTOR. HIS NAME IS RAYMOND KESSLER.

YES. CALL ME BACK TOMORROW. I'LL DO MY BEST.

THAT'S ALL YOU CAN DO, MY FRIEND.

15

IT'S ALL **ANY** OF US CAN DO.

GIGHHHH...

RRRING

...MM?

HELLO?

DIAN, THANK **GOD** YOU'RE THERE. I HAVE TO TALK TO SOMEONE, I--

LISTEN, LUCY, I'M NOT REALLY **AWAKE** YET. COULD I CALL YOU BACK--

HE **HURT** ME, DIAN.

WHAT? **WHO** HURT YOU?

RAY...AND I...WE... HAD SOME...TROUBLE LAST NIGHT. I DON'T KNOW IF I'M ALL RIGHT...

MY GOD, LUCY. WHERE **ARE** YOU?

AT RAY'S, HE... I JUST DIDN'T KNOW WHERE TO GO--

LUCY, I'M COMING **RIGHT** OVER THERE TO GET YOU.

DIAN...COULD YOU... B-BRING ME A DRESS AND SOME STOCKINGS?

OH DEAR GOD. I WILL. NOW GIVE ME THE ADDRESS--

There's always some sort of balance, isn't there?

Just when you're certain that your life is as bad as can be--

DIAN?

--you're shown a glimpse of how much worse things could go.

I'M *HERE,* HONEY! IT'S *OKAY!*

COME IN.

I APPRECIATE THIS, DIAN. AND I'M *SORRY* TO PULL YOU INTO IT. I-I REALLY THOUGHT RAY WAS A *DIFFERENT* MAN THAN HE IS!

BELIEVE ME, HONEY, I *KNOW* HOW THAT CAN BE.

BUT DON'T THINK A THING OF IT. WE'RE *FAMILY.* AND FAMILY *HELPS* FAMILY.

NOT RAY'S. HIS GODDAMN *SON* IS THE ONE WHO BROUGHT THIS ALL OUT OF HIM.

I GUESS I JUST GOT CAUGHT IN THE *MIDDLE* OF THEIR ANGER.

THAT BOY IS *NOTHING* BUT TROUBLE. DO YOU KNOW THAT LAST NIGHT WHEN I GOT HERE, HE EVEN HAD THE GALL TO *LOCK* THIS DOOR?

THE NERVE. AS IF I WOULD EVER *STEAL* SOMETHING FROM R-R-RAAAAY--

U-HUH-HUH OH, RAY... WHY...?

HERE, COME ON, LUCY. IT'S GOING TO BE ALL RIGHT.

LET'S GET YOU *OUT* OF HERE.

17

--THANK YOU, YOU'VE BEEN **SO** KIND, AND AFTER I SAID SUCH CATTY THINGS ABOUT YOUR WESLEY.

I MUST REALLY LOOK THE FOOL.

NO, NOT AT ALL. WESLEY HAS HIS SHORTCOMINGS AS WELL.

NOW TELL ME, WHAT BROUGHT ON THIS HORRIBLE BEHAVIOR OF RAY'S? YOU SAID IT WAS HIS **SON**?

OH, I DON'T KNOW. IT'S REALLY **MY** FAULT. I USED HIS KEY TO GET IN WHEN I SHOULDN'T HAVE, AND THEN, RAY WAS...**AMOROUS**, AND I TOLD HIM "NO."

I--I SHOULD HAVE JUST--

WELL, RAY **ALWAYS** GETS WHAT HE WANTS IN THE END--

YOU MEAN HE **RAPED YOU**, LUCY?

I--I DON'T KNOW THAT I'D CALL IT **THAT**, BUT...

OH, DIAN, THERE'S NO NEED TO GET RILED UP ON MY BEHALF.

AFTER ALL, I DE-SERVED IT.

IF I **REALLY** LOVED HIM, I'D BE MORE...UNDER-STANDING, WOULDN'T I?

LUCY, WHAT RAY DID WAS **WRONG**. I THINK YOU SHOULD--

I WILL, DIAN, **TOMORROW** I'LL APOLOGIZE.

APOLO--?! LUCY!

BUT FOR RIGHT NOW WOULD YOU MIND IF I HAD A **NAP**?

I STILL NEED TO RETURN THAT HOUSE KEY. I'M BUSHED.

DO YOU KNOW THAT LAST NIGHT I EVEN DREAMT THAT A MAN IN A **GAS MASK** CAME INTO OUR ROOM?

HAVE YOU EVER **HEARD** OF SUCH A THING?

A GAS MASK?

YEAH. CRAZY, HUH?

YOU REST AS LONG AS YOU LIKE, LUCY. I'LL WAKE YOU LATER.

Much later.

18

EXCUSE ME, SIR?

--HUH--?

IT'S *PAST FIVE, SIR.* I THOUGHT I SHOULD WAKE YOU.

PAST FIVE? GOOD HEAVENS, I'VE SLEPT ALL--

HUMPHRIES, COULD YOU FRY ME AN OMELET? I'M GOING TO MAKE A FEW CALLS, SHOWER, AND I'LL BE RIGHT DOWN.

CERTAINLY, SIR.

RING RING

THERE YOU ARE.

CORONER'S OFFICE, THIS IS HUBERT SPEAKING.

HUBERT KLEIN, THIS IS THE SANDMAN.

HAVE YOU DISCOVERED THE ANSWER TO MY QUERY?

THE LICENSE LOOKS SUSPICIOUS. I DID SOME DIGGING, THROUGH MY MEDICAL ASSOCIATES, ON THIS *"DR."* KESSLER. QUITE A QUACK, APPARENTLY.

DOES LITTLE MORE THAN DOLE OUT *NERVE PILLS* TO SOCIETY MATRONS. ONLY MAKES HOUSE CALLS. VERY SHADY.

TELL WHAT YOU HAVE LEARNED TO THE PROPER AUTHORITIES.

CONVINCE THEM TO SEARCH KESSLER'S OFFICES FOR RROOF AND THEN PROCEED TO HIS HOUSE.

I WILL. ENSURE DR. DEATH WRITES NO MORE PRESCRIPTIONS.

19

Lucy's story did nothing to bring any new light to my confusion over Wesley--

HM...

--But it did plenty to convince me that there's something more to Ray's behavior than a troublesome *son*.

Heaven knows I give daddy no end of confusion--

--But he would never go so far as to attack *anyone*.

THERE YOU ARE.

There has to be some greater reason.

KI-CHAK

Extreme behavior has to have equally strong motivations behind it.

20

GOODNIGHT.

GOOD NIGHT? YOU TOLD ME WE WERE GOING *OUT* TONIGHT, RAY.

MAYBE WE *WILL.* I'LL GIVE YOU A CALL LATER IF MY EVENING OPENS UP.

YOUR EVENING MIGHT, BUT *I* SURE WON'T. GOOD *NIGHT,* MR. KESSLER.

THAT'S *DOCTOR* KESSLER, ARLENE.

WHATEVER YOU SAY... *DOCTOR.*

"MISTER."   BITCH.

People do what they're driven to do...

...what they must do.

Maybe that's what Wesley was trying to say...

WHAT--?

21

ROMAN? IS DAT YOU? MOMMA VUNTS--

ROMAN? NO? IS RAYMOND? HONEY, PLEASE GIFF MOMMA HER SHOT...NOW--

MA'AM? I...I'M SORRY TO INTRUDE. I --

--PLEASE, HONEY, YOU FORGOT AGAIN--

VUNT TO FEEL BETTER...NOT SO COLD UND STIFF--BITTE, MEIN KINDER, RAYMOND FORGOT... RAYMOND--

RAYMOND DID THIS TO YOU? HIS OWN MOTHER?

YOU'RE... RAYMOND'S MOTHER?

WHO...? WHO IS DER? VAT DO YOU VUNT? PLEASE--I AM ONLY OLD WOMAN...

MA'AM, LISTEN TO ME. I'M SORRY, BUT I CAN'T GIVE YOU THAT SHOT. I WILL GO GET SOME HELP FOR YOU THOUGH. I--I PROMISE.

But in the greater balance of things, no matter how strong the motivation--

--there are some behaviors that simply CAN'T be justified.

22

OH!

WHAT IN THE FUCK WERE *YOU* DOING UP THERE?! WHAT ARE YOU DOING IN MY *HOUSE*?

I COULD ASK *YOU* THE SAME QUESTIONS. THAT WOMAN UPSTAIRS IS--IS-- IT'S LIKE A LIVING *DEATH*!

IT'S WORSE THAN DEATH, SWEETHEART. TO BE OLD AND IN PAIN... WEAK LIKE A BABY.

THAT'S NO WAY TO LIVE!

WHY, I'D PUT 'EM *ALL* DOWN IF I COULD.

AND YET YOUR MOTHER LINGERS IN DELIRIUM...

< GASP >

CLIK

KILL MY OWN MOTHER...?

YOU STUPID GODDAMN BITCH!

AGHH!

CRACK

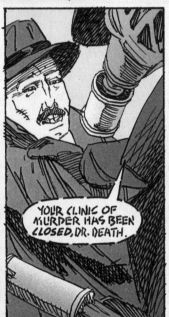

YOUR CLINIC OF MURDER HAS BEEN CLOSED, DR. DEATH.

LICENSE REVOKED.

NO! I WAS DOING THEM A FAVOR! THEIR LIVES WERE MISERABLE--POINTLESS. THEY JUST SADDLED ME-- US WITH DEAD WEIGHT. I--

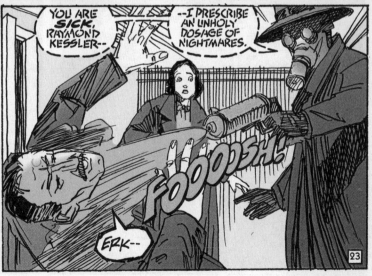

YOU ARE *SICK*, RAYMOND KESSLER--

--I PRESCRIBE AN UNHOLY DOSAGE OF NIGHTMARES.

ERK--

FOOOOSH!

23

ARE YOU ALL RIGHT?

I--I--

It's all so complicated, life.

It's one thing one moment--

--And the next--

--Something else entirely.

THE POLICE APPROACH. I MUST GO.

(cough!)

Familiar at first sight--

OPEN UP! POLICE!

--And utterly unknowable the next.

BELMONT? WHAT IN GOD'S NAME ARE YOU DOING HERE?

HE TRIED TO KILL ME.

MY CONDOLENCES, BUT THAT SURE AS SHIT DOESN'T ANSWER MY QUESTION.

YOU'VE GOT A HELLUVA LOT OF EXPLAININ' TO DO. D.A.'S DAUGHTER OR NOT, I DON'T LIKE FINDING YOU AT THE SCENE OF EVERY BUST I MAKE, YOUNG LADY!

DON'T WORRY, LIEUTENANT BURKE, IT WON'T HAPPEN AGAIN.

I PROMISE YOU IT WON'T.

DAMN STRAIGHT, AND-- HEY! WHAT'S THAT I SMELL...?

THE END

-THE NIGHT- OF THE -BUTCHER-

WRITTEN BY MATT WAGNER
AND STEVEN T. SEAGLE

ART BY GUY DAVIS

LETTERING BY JOHN COSTANZA

OR IS THERE NO EGRESS FROM THIS JIGSAW OF IMAGES?

"This puzzle is

the man whole,

yet in pieces.

Is there a way to fuse

the pieces

and make the man?"

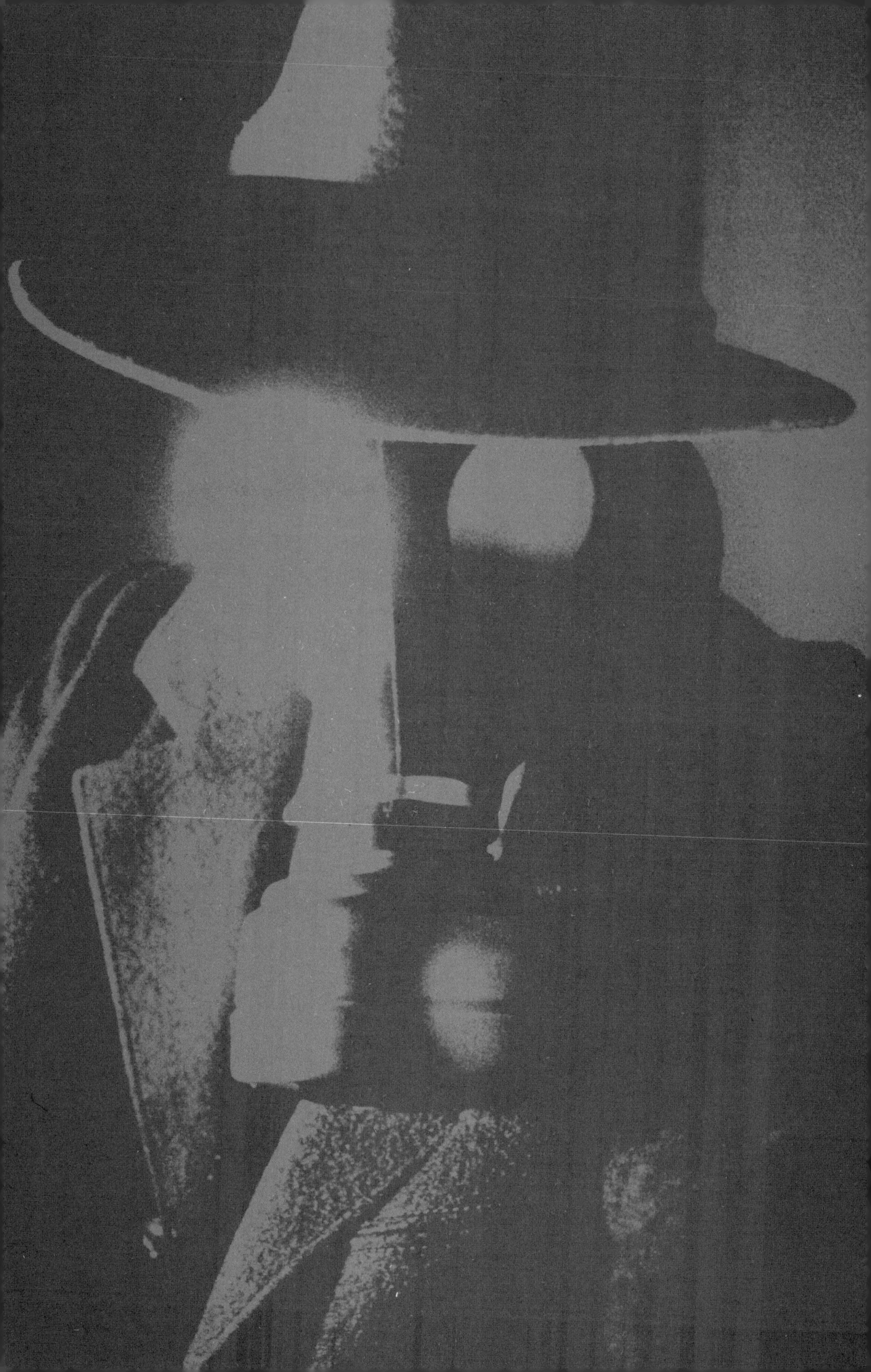

EACH DAY BEGINS WITH THE CRIES, THE GASPS FOR BREATH, THE END OF REST.

AND THEN THEY COME, POISED, NEEDLING, PIERCING.

YOU LIE BEFORE THEM VULNERABLE, NAKED, DEFENSELESS.

BUT EVEN THAT PRONE STATE OF HELPLESSNESS IS NOT ENOUGH--

THEY WANT MORE, THE INSIDE, THE CONCEALED, THE HIDDEN.

AND WHEN YOU DON'T OFFER, THEY SEARCH, PROD, DISCOVER.

NO MATTER HOW DEEPLY IT IS CONCEALED, THEY WILL FIND IT.

NO MATTER WHAT YOU DO TO SUPPRESS IT, IT WILL BE UNCOVERED.

AND YOU WILL STAND UNMASKED, YOUR TRUE SELF ONCE MORE...

AESCHYLUS WROTE ABOUT IT--

--I DO KNOW THE FACE--I KNOW IT! STOP TORTURING ME--

MASTER DODDS! TRY TO RELAX, SIR. YOU'VE HAD A PARTICULARLY BAD EPISODE, BUT IT IS OVER NOW.

IT'S ALL OVER.

MY GOD, HUMPHRIES, HOW I WISH YOU WERE RIGHT--

--BUT IT'S NOT OVER. IT'S HAPPENING AGAIN.

--THE NEED TO EXPRESS THE INWARD SELF OUTWARDLY.

BUT THE DREAM... THE FACE I SAW WAS--WAS--

--I HAVE TO CALL DIAN. TALK TO HER. HAS SHE CALLED?

NO, SIR, NOT FOR DAYS.

SHE SAW IT, HUMPHRIES. THE LABORATORY. SHE KNOWS ABOUT HIM... ABOUT ME.

SHE SAID THAT SHE--THAT--

--SIGH...COFFEE, PLEASE, HUMPHRIES, BLACK. I'LL BE DOWN IN A MOMENT.

YES, SIR.

HOW SIMPLE IT MUST BE TO PHILOSOPHIZE--

2

--TO STAND AT THE PINNACLE--

--GAZING INTO THE VERTIGINOUS MAW OF A GREAT CHASM--

--AND THEN SIMPLY JOT DOWN ONE'S CONCLUSIONS.

THE SAFETY OF THE THEORETICAL CONSTRUCT--

--KEEPING ONE ARM'S LENGTH FROM A COLD PLUNGE INTO THE BRUTAL TRUTH BEHIND THE THOUGHT.

DEDUCTIONS DRAWN FROM PRESUMPTION--

--WITHOUT EVER REALLY CROSSING THE VALE INTO THE REALITY THOSE ASSERTIONS CLAIM TO ADDRESS.

I'VE ALWAYS HATED AESCHYLUS.

3

NIGHT OF THE BUTCHER
ACT·ONE

ARTIE? BEEN A DOG OF A DAY. YOU CAN IMPROVE IT BY HITTIN' 'A WHISKEY TO THE BAR SO THAT *IT* LANDS THERE WHEN *I* DO.

NAH NAH NAH, YER ALL WORKED UP OVER *NOTHING.* BESIDES, THAT'S *EUROPE.* WHADDA WE CARE ABOUT EUROPE? IT'S A MILLION MILES FROM HERE.

CHRIST WOULDA SPIT ON THE APOSTLES IF HE'D HAD MY DAY.

I'LL MAKE IT A *DOUBLE,* THEN.

DOUBLE *THEN?* MAKE IT A DOUBLE *NOW.*

HA! HEY, BURKE, THAT'S A *GOOD* ONE.

YEAH, I GOT A *TON* OF 'EM, SULLIVAN.

Y'KNOW, WE WERE JUST TALKIN' ABOUT HITLER--

4

LOOK, I'M TELLIN' YA, THE KOOK UP AND TOOK THE RHINELAND, AND THEN *AUSTRIA*. WHAT'S NEXT? HUH?

BLACK ONE TODAY, *HUH*, LIEUTENANT?

YEAH? WELL *STOP* IT!

HAW HAW HAW HAW!

HERE'S ONE FOR YOU HYENAS--

--THIS LONG ISLAND BROAD WANTS TO HAVE MORE TIME WITH HER HUSBAND, SO SHE UP AND HIRES A MAID. POLISH, BIG TITS, BIG ASS, NICE PACKAGE ALL AROUND.

SO AFTER A FEW WEEKS, THIS BROAD GETS THE FEELING HER HUSBAND'S FALLIN' FOR THE HELP, BUT SHE DOESN'T WANNA COME RIGHT OUT AND SAY IT, SO SHE ASKS HIM--

"CHARLES, DO YOU THINK A MAN CAN LOVE *TWO* GIRLS AT THE SAME TIME?"

AND HE SAYS, "SURE! INVITE HER UP WITH US TONIGHT!"

HAW HAW HAW HAW

HEH HEH HEH. HELL, WHY NOT? HE PAYS HER *SALARY,* DOESN'T HE?!

5

ROLLO? MOMMA'S HOME, HONEY.

RARF ARF ARF!

YAH, SHWEETY. MOMMA LOVES YOU TOO.

RARF!

CHUST A MINUTE... LET MOMMA TAKE CARE OF HER WRAP.

EXCITED BOY, YOU'RE HAPPY TO HAVE MOMMA BACK? MOMMA'S GLAD TO BE BACK. THOSE MEN... SCHIESS!

RRRR RARF! RARF!

OHHH... AND NOW SO GRUMPY, HONEY? YOU WANT A TREAT?

RRRRRR...

6

ALL RIGHT, LET MOMMA SEE WHAT SHE GOT FOR YOU TODAY.

RRRRRRR

ROLLO! THERE'S NO CALL TO BE MEAN. YOU STOP THAT.

RARF! RARF!

MOMMA'S NOT GOING TO FEED YOU IF--

CHOK

RARF

SWUNK

CHOK

CHOK

RIIING RIIING

--HUH...?

RIIING RIIING

YEAH, YES? HUMPHRIES?

YES. BEGGING YOUR *PARDON*, SIR, BUT JUDGE SCHAEFFER IS HERE TO SEE YOU. I THOUGHT I MIGHT TELL HIM YOU WERE *ASLEEP*, BUT UNDER THE CIRCUMSTANCES I THOUGHT YOU MIGHT APPRECIATE THE COMPANY.

YES, HUMPHRIES, GOOD THOUGHT. I'LL BE...UM, RIGHT UP.

SOME MEN SEEM TO LIVE SO EASILY, CHARTING THEIR OWN COURSE.

NOT SO MUCH STEERING CLEAR OF THE DANGEROUS REEFS--

--AS SIMPLY CHOOSING NOT TO EVEN ACKNOWLEDGE THEIR EXISTENCE.

SORRY TO HAVE KEPT YOU WAITING *AGAIN*, JUDGE SCHAEFFER.

THERE'S THE GOLDEN BOY!

AND STOP CALLING ME "JUDGE." EASE UP A BIT. I ALWAYS FEEL LIKE I'M IN THE COURTROOM WHEN I'M TALKING TO YOU.

DON'T TAKE IT PERSONALLY, I EVEN CALLED MY *FATHER* "MR. DODDS."

KEEN WIT'S THE SIGN OF A GOOD LOVE LIFE. YOU *MUST* BE SATISFIED IN THAT DEPARTMENT.

OR *YOU* MUST BE A POOR JUDGE OF WIT.

8

THINGS *WERE* GOING WELL... IN *THAT* DEPARTMENT... BUT NOW DIAN'S WITHDRAWN. SHE THINKS I'M NOT BEING *GENUINE* ENOUGH WITH HER

HARBORING *SECRETS,* EH? WELL... *ARE* YOU?

HUH? WELL... WELL I *SUPPOSE* I AM. A *FEW.*

BUT ACKNOWLEDGED OR NOT--

WELL WHO THE HELL *DOESN'T,* MY BOY?

THAT'S PART OF THE *GAME.* IF YOU EACH KNEW EVERYTHING ABOUT THE OTHER, IT WOULDN'T MATTER ANYMORE.

BUT HOW DO YOU DECIDE WHAT YOU SHOULD AND SHOULDN'T SHARE?

THAT'S *EASY.* SHARE EVERYTHING SHE *WANTS* TO HEAR, AND NOTHING SHE *DOESN'T.*

SOUNDS LIKE THE LEAGUE OF NATIONS.

EXACTLY. KEEN WIT, I'M TELLIN' YOU!

AND SPEAKING OF WIT, OR SHOULD I SAY *LACK* OF...

...REMEMBER THAT VIGILANTE I TOLD YOU ABOUT? WITH THE GAS AND ALL? SEEMS THE PRECINCT BOYS'VE GIVEN HIM A SILLY CODE NAME NOW.

"THE SANDMAN."

CAN YOU BELIEVE *THAT* ONE?

I CAN'T SAY.

--THOSE DANGERS ARE STILL OUT THERE.

WHAT'S IT *LIKE* IN THERE, BOYD?

LIKE A MEAT MARKET, LIEUTENANT.

SHIT.

WHO'S THE *DIGGER?*

LUCIO CARDINO. HE'S THE MANAGER.

YOU SEE ANYTHING, LUKE?

I DON' WANT *ANY* TROUBLE HERE. I RENT ONLY TO *NICE PEOPLE* HERE.

THIS A NICE PLACE. ONLY NICE PEOPLE.

NICE PEOPLE WHO CAN'T AFFORD A POT TO *PISS* IN MAYBE.

DON'T YOU GO ANYWHERE, LUKE. I MIGHT WANT TO ASK YOU SOME MORE QUESTIONS--

--AFTER I GET A LOOK AT THE *"NICE PERSON"* WHO JUST HAPPENED TO GET--

JESUS FUCKING MARY AND JOSEPH!

JUSTIFICATIONS--

THAT'S WHAT MAN TRULY SEEKS THROUGH METAPHYSICAL PURSUITS.

THANKS FOR COMING BY. IT WAS JUST THE LIFT I NEEDED TODAY.

WESLEY, DON'T LET THIS GET YOU TOO FAR DOWN. SHE'LL COME AROUND. JUST TAKES TIME.

IT'LL ALL COME OUT LIKE YOU WANT IT TO IF YOU *MAKE* IT HAPPEN. SEE YOU SOON.

THAT WAS A LENGTHY VISIT. SHOULD I PUT DINNER OUT FOR YOU NOW?

NO. NO THANK YOU, HUMPHRIES. NOT JUST YET.

I'VE GOT A SUDDEN BURST OF ENERGY, AND I WANT TO PUT IT TO GOOD USE.

ONE LOOKS FOR SOME IMPORTANT BACKING FOR WHY HE DOES WHAT HE DOES--

--WHY OTHERS FOLLOW THEIR COURSES, INEVITABLY DIFFER-ENT FROM HIS OWN--

--AND WHAT LIES IN THE SPACE BETWEEN THE TWO.

HELLO, LARRY. WESLEY DODDS CALLING. HOW ARE YOU?... GOOD, GOOD... IS DIAN ABOUT?

WHY NO. SHE'S OUT, *HAS* BEEN THE LAST SEVERAL NIGHTS. I'D ASSUMED SHE WAS OUT WITH YOU--ER... THAT IS...

I UNDERSTAND, LARRY. THANKS. IF YOU COULD TELL HER I *CALLED?*... UH-HUH, I WILL ...GOODBYE.

11

ALL VERY SOUND--

-- BUT WHERE DOES THAT LEAVE THE HEART?

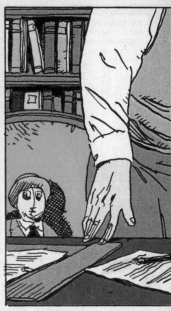

I'M TELLIN' YA, IT WAS ALL I COULD DO TO LOOK AT IT, GEORGE, AN' I'VE SEEN SOME REAL BAD SHIT IN MY TIME.

COME.

TAP TAP

ABOUT TIME. WHAT YA GOT FOR US, HUEY?

ASIDE FROM THE OBVIOUS, THAT IS.

LIEUTENANT BURKE... I MUST SAY THAT IN ALL MY YEARS OF FORENSIC DISCOVERY, I HAVE NEVER SEEN ANYTHING SO DISTURBING. THE SHEER UNBRIDLED--

FOR ONCE, I'M WITH YOU. NOW GET YAPPIN'!

AS YOU'LL SEE FROM THE PHOTOS--

PHOTOS--?

--THE CAUSE OF DEATH WAS SEVERANCE OF THE SPINAL COLUMN.

IT APPEARS THE HEAD WAS THE FIRST--

HOLY SHIT! WHATTYA GOTTA DO TO GET SOMETHIN' LIKE *THAT* DONE TO YOU?

MAYBE JUST BE A BROAD. SHE PROBABLY GOT SOME GUY ALL HOT IN THE TROUSERS THEN PUSHED HIM OFF.

HEY, IN THAT CASE, I'D KNOW HOW HE FELT. SOMETIMES MY WIFE'S A REAL PRICKTEASE. I *HATE* THAT--

OR MAYBE IT WAS BECAUSE SHE WAS A JEW.

HER NAME, IN CASE YOU *CARE*, WAS HIRSCHEL. RUTH HIRSCHEL.

GIVEN THE WORLD SITUATION, I THINK IT MIGHT BE--

AHH--LEAVE THAT SHIT TO THE KRAUTS. 'SIDES, SHE SEEMS TO HAVE BEEN A REAL LONER, TOO. TELL ME MORE ABOUT THE CHOP JOB.

WELL...THE HEAD WAS SEVERED IN TWO BLOWS. THE FIRST WAS NEARLY COMPLETE, THE SECOND FINISHED THE JOB.

THE REMAINING LIMBS WERE MOSTLY SINGLE AND DOUBLE CUTS. WHOEVER DID THIS WAS *INCREDIBLY* STRONG.

I HAVE NO IDEA WHY THE PARTICULAR CHOICES FOR SEVERANCE WERE MADE--

--AND SO FAR, WE'VE YET TO RECOVER ALL THE PARTS.

WE DO HAVE THE HEAD THOUGH... THUS THE I.D..

GO ON.

13

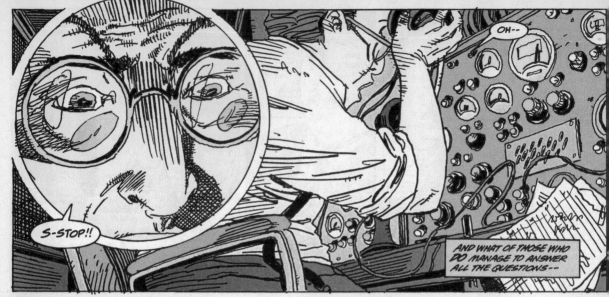

OH--

S-STOP!!

AND WHAT OF THOSE WHO *DO* MANAGE TO ANSWER ALL THE QUESTIONS--

--OH, GOD--

--AND ARRIVE AT SOME SENSE OF EQUILIBRIUM?

HU-HORRK SPATT

WHAT DO THEY THEN DO--

--WHEN SOMETHING INCONSISTENT WITH THEIR BALANCED VIEWS COMES ALONG?

UNNNNN...

DOES IT FORCE THEM RIGHT BACK INTO CHAOS?

COUNTERACT ALL THE "PROGRESS" THEY'VE MADE?

OR DO THEY IGNORE IT BECAUSE THEY DECIDE THAT IT'S TOO HORRIBLE TO COMPREHEND SOMETHING THAT FAR AFIELD OF THEIR ESTABLISHED LIVES?

...AND WHERE HAVE YOU HEARD THAT BEFORE, WES?

14

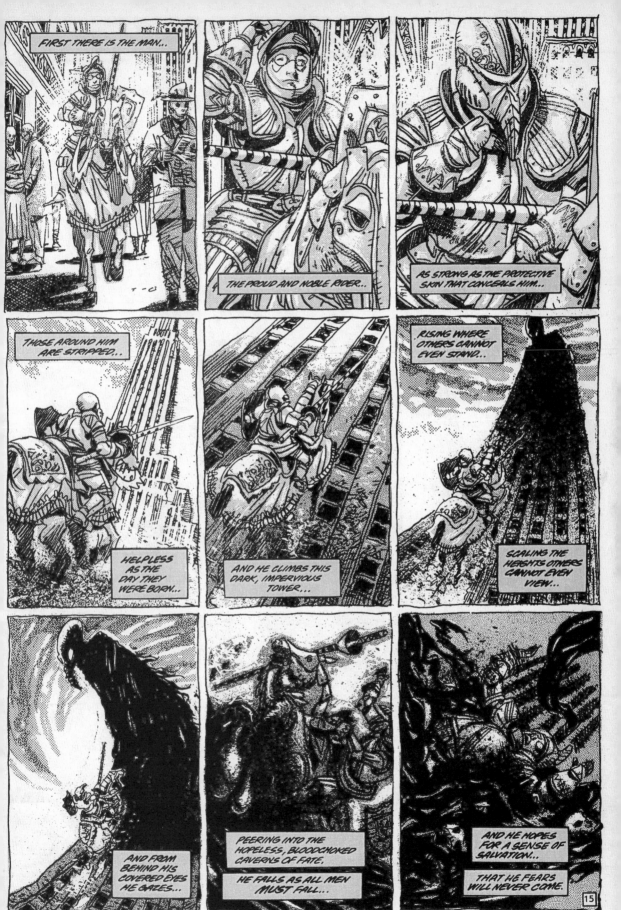

FIRST THERE IS THE MAN...

THE PROUD AND NOBLE RIDER...

AS STRONG AS THE PROTECTIVE SKIN THAT CONCEALS HIM...

THOSE AROUND HIM ARE STRIPPED...

HELPLESS AS THE DAY THEY WERE BORN...

AND HE CLIMBS THIS DARK, IMPERVIOUS TOWER...

RISING WHERE OTHERS CANNOT EVEN STAND...

SCALING THE HEIGHTS OTHERS CANNOT EVEN VIEW...

AND FROM BEHIND HIS COVERED EYES HE GAZES...

PEERING INTO THE HOPELESS, BLOODCHOKED CAVERNS OF FATE,

HE FALLS AS ALL MEN MUST FALL...

AND HE HOPES FOR A SENSE OF SALVATION...

THAT HE FEARS WILL NEVER COME.

15

RrRr Rrrrrrrrng

RrRr Rrrrrrrrng

DAMN IT!

WHY THE HELL ARE YOU *CALLING* ME AT THIS TIME OF THE MORNING, WHO THE HELL ARE YOU, AND WHAT THE HELL DO YOU *WANT?*

UM... LIEUTENANT BURKE? THIS IS RAWLEY, ON THE NIGHT BEAT. I LOST THE DRAW TO CALL YOU, *UH--*

--WE GOT A *BAD* SITUATION ON THE EASTSIDE. THERE'S A BODY STUFFED IN THE SEWER HERE.

IF THERE AIN'T *MORE* TO THIS STORY, THERE'S GONNA BE *ANOTHER* BODY STUFFED IN THE SEWER ON *TOP* OF THAT ONE.

AW, C'MON, LIEUTENANT. THIS GUY REALLY STINKS, LIKE HE'S *ROTTED*, BUT WHAT WE CAN SEE OF HIM SAYS HE CAN'T HAVE BEEN DEAD THAT LONG.

PLUS WE GOT SOME BRUISER PATROL-MEN FROM ACROSS THE RIVER TRYIN' T' TELL US THIS AIN'T OUR JURISDICTION--

THERE AIN'T MUCH I HATE MORE THAN BEIN' WOKEN UP, BUT COPS FROM QUEENS WOULD BE RIGHT UP THERE.

ALL RIGHT, RAWLEY, I'M COMIN'. GIVE ME SOME CROSS STREETS.

UH HUH.

BASTARDS COULDN'T SCRATCH THEMSELVES WITHOUT A SPARE SET OF HANDS...

CLK

16

118

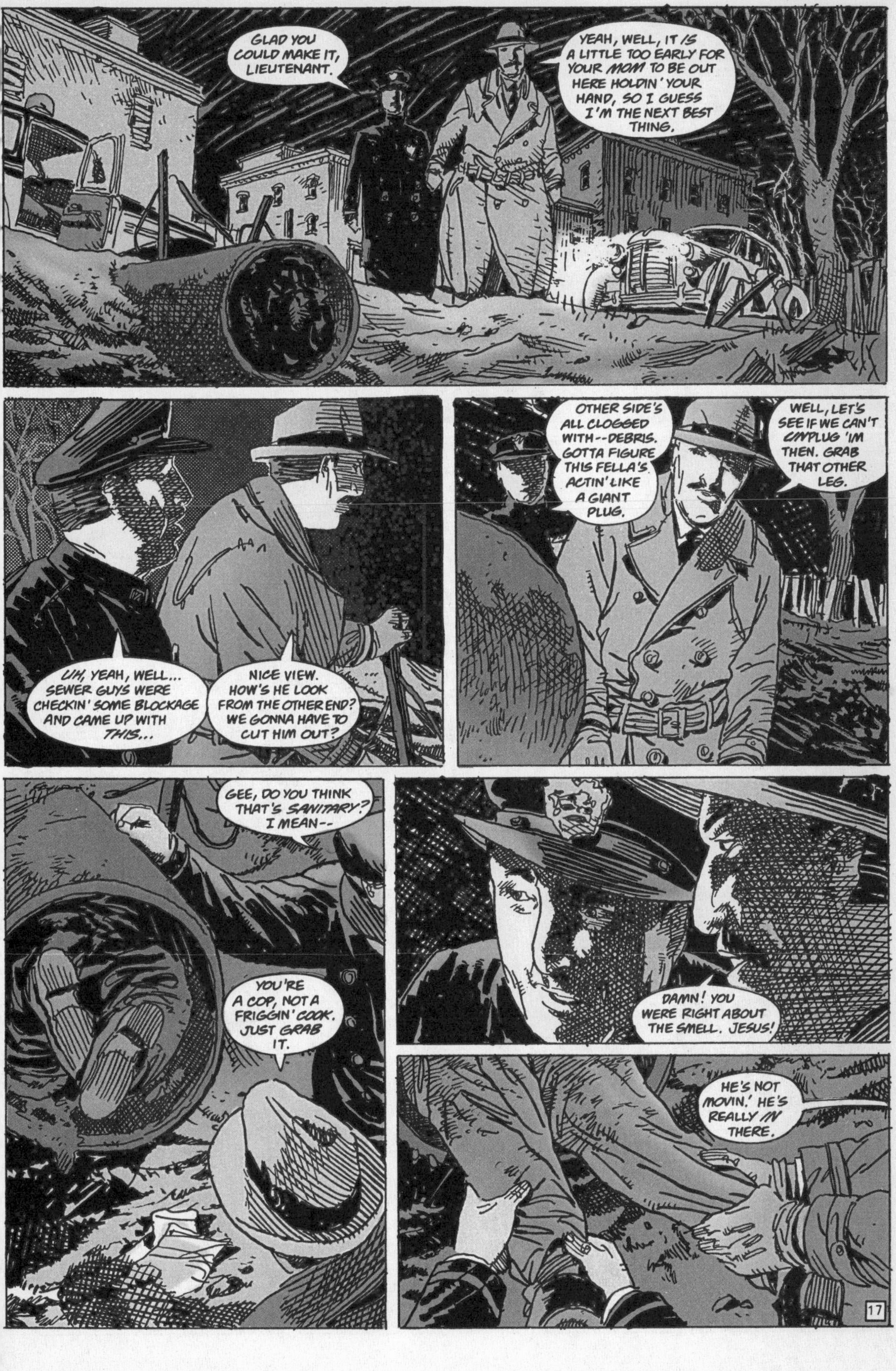
GLAD YOU COULD MAKE IT, LIEUTENANT.
YEAH, WELL, IT IS A LITTLE TOO EARLY FOR YOUR MOM TO BE OUT HERE HOLDIN' YOUR HAND, SO I GUESS I'M THE NEXT BEST THING.
UH, YEAH, WELL... SEWER GUYS WERE CHECKIN' SOME BLOCKAGE AND CAME UP WITH THIS...
NICE VIEW. HOW'S HE LOOK FROM THE OTHER END? WE GONNA HAVE TO CUT HIM OUT?
OTHER SIDE'S ALL CLOGGED WITH--DEBRIS. GOTTA FIGURE THIS FELLA'S ACTIN' LIKE A GIANT PLUG.
WELL, LET'S SEE IF WE CAN'T UNPLUG 'IM THEN. GRAB THAT OTHER LEG.
GEE, DO YOU THINK THAT'S SANITARY? I MEAN--
YOU'RE A COP, NOT A FRIGGIN' COOK. JUST GRAB IT.
DAMN! YOU WERE RIGHT ABOUT THE SMELL. JESUS!
HE'S NOT MOVIN.' HE'S REALLY IN THERE.
17

PULL HARDER, HE'S *GOTTA* GIVE.

PULL, DAMN IT!

HE'S *COMIN'*!

SPLORCH

UNHHH!

WHOA-- SHIT!

FUCKING HELL! ANOTHER HALF-ER? WHAT *IS* THIS SHIT?

OH MY GOD! OH MY GOD! WHAT *HAPPENED* TO HIM?

DOESN'T TAKE MUCH OF A DETECTIVE TO SEE THAT HE'S BEEN CHOPPED IN HALF, WHICH IS LUCKY, SINCE YOU OBVIOUSLY AREN'T MUCH OF A DETECTIVE.

GOD THAT'S HORRIBLE--

SURE IS. NOT ONLY ARE THESE NEW TROUSERS--

--BUT THOSE LOOK LIKE THE SAME HACK MARKS WE FOUND ON THE WOMAN DOWNTOWN YESTERDAY.

18

DIDN'T I ALREADY SIGN THIS, JOYCE?

NOT YET, MR. DODDS. IF YOU'D ALREADY SIGNED IT, I WOULDN'T BE ASKING YOU TO SIGN IT.

NO, I SUPPOSE NOT.

AND WHEN YOU'RE DONE WITH THAT ONE, YOU CAN KEEP THAT PEN CAP OFF. THESE *MUST* GO OUT TODAY.

WHAT? YOU'RE JOKING.

YOU'RE *NOT* JOKING. WELL... I'M SORRY, BUT I CAN'T DO ALL THIS TODAY.

REALLY.

I CERTAINLY CAN'T *MAKE* YOU, BUT DON'T COME CRYING TO ME WHEN YOUR COMPANY FALLS APART.

I'LL BE OUTSIDE IF YOU NEED ME.

IF I NEED YOU...

....IF I NEED YOU...

I DON'T KNOW WHAT I NEED, JOYCE.

BZZT. MR. DODDS? THERE'S A ROBERT LI HERE TO SEE YOU?

REALLY? SUPER. SHOW HIM RIGHT IN.

19

ROBERT! WHAT A **SURPRISE** THIS IS. COME TO DUKE IT OUT OVER THAT NEWS-PAPER STUNT OF MINE?

NOT AT ALL--

--JUST THOUGHT I'D RETURN THE FAVOR AND DROP IN ON **YOU** UNEXPECTEDLY.

HOW'RE YOU DOING?

OH, FINE... I SUPPOSE.

NOW IF I REMEMBER OUR COLLEGE DAYS CORRECTLY--AND I'M CERTAIN I **DO**--

--ANY TIME YOU USE THE DEPENDENT CLAUSE "**I SUPPOSE**" YOU'RE **ACTUALLY** NEGATING WHATEVER CAME **BEFORE.**

HAVE YOU EVER CONSIDERED A CAREER IN **DETECTION**, ROBERT? YOU SEEM TO PERCEIVE QUITE A LOT.

HA! TOO FRANTIC FOR **MY** BLOOD. NOW **TELL** ME, WHATEVER'S WRONG?

IT'S MY GIRLFRIEND, DIAN. WE'VE HAD A FALLING OUT THAT WE MAY NOT GET OVER.

ROBERT'S RULE NUMBER **ONE**: THERE IS NOTHING A MAN CAN'T GET OVER.

ROBERT'S RULE NUMBER **TWO**: NOTHING CURES THE BLUES LIKE AN EVENING IN MARVELOUS MANHATTAN.

YOU THINK SO?

I KNOW SO. COME ON!

AT THIS POINT... I SUPPOSE IT'S FAIR TO SAY I'LL TRY **ANY**-THING.

20

LOOK, PAL, I'M NOT ASKIN' YA T'DO ANYTHING *ILLEGAL.* I'M A POLICE OFFICER. REMEMBER?

NOW GIMME THE DAMNED *PASS-KEY,* OR I'M *KICKIN'* HER DOOR DOWN.

YES, YES... NO TROUBLE, PLEASE. HERE IS KEY.

SHEESH.

HM.

TOO SMALL...

...NOTHIN' WRONG HERE...

21

....AIN'T BEEN OPENED IN YEARS...

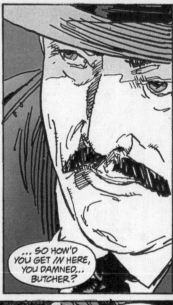

... SO HOW'D YOU GET *IN* HERE, YOU DAMNED... BUTCHER?

WAIT A MINUTE...

WHEW-- FUCKING PITS!

SMELLS LIKE A SEWER.

HM.

22

YOU *KNOW* THIS PLACE, ROBERT? IT DOESN'T *LOOK* LIKE YOU.

THINGS ARE SOMETIMES *MORE* THAN THEY APPEAR.

I'VE BEEN HERE ONCE BE--

EVENING SIR.

IS THERE A PROBLEM?

NO PROBLEM.

WE'RE JUST A BIT FULL UP HERE IS ALL. YOU BOY'S SHOULD PROBABLY GO FIND SOMEPLACE *ELSE*.

DAMN...

FULL UP? THERE'S NO ONE *WAITING*.

I SAID WE'RE FULL UP, MR. MOTO.

LOOK, GENTLEMEN, I'VE JUST HAD A FALLING OUT WITH MY GIRL. I DON'T *WANT* TO GO ANYWHERE ELSE.

NOW MY FRIEND AND I INTEND TO SPEND A *LOT* OF MONEY HERE TONIGHT. AND I'M NOT AGAINST STARTING THAT SPENDING HERE WITH *YOU*.

FURTHERMORE, I IMAGINE THAT THE HOUSE LIGHTS ARE LOW ENOUGH THAT IF WE SAT IN THE BACK, WE'D HARDLY BE *NOTICED*.

YEAH, THE BACK IS FINE. HAVE A GOOD EVENING.

...PLEASANT DREAMS...

23

SORRY ABOUT THAT MESS.

--NO, IT'S NOT *YOUR* FAULT. THOSE MUSCLE HEADS PROBABLY DON'T EVEN KNOW THE DIFFERENCE BETWEEN THE CHINESE AND THE JAPANESE. FORGET 'EM.

HI, GENTS, NAME YOUR POISON.

BEER... FOR *BOTH* OF US.

BUT I--

STILL DON'T DRINK MUCH? YOU DO TONIGHT, *"BROTHER."*

LISTEN TO THAT JAZZ. THAT IS *HOT*.

ARE YOU SURE IT'S THE *JAZZ*, OR THE THERMOSTAT IN HERE ON THE BLINK?

DO I DETECT A JOKE FROM *"STONEFACE"* DODDS?

I GUESS YOU DO--

--AND I GUESS YOU WERE RIGHT. I REALLY DID NEED TO GET OUT.

--I *OWE* YOU ONE. THANKS.

EH?

I ALWAYS COLLECT ON MY DEBTS. I *AM* CHINESE AFTER ALL... IN CASE YOU HADN'T NOTICED! HA HA!

D-DIAN...?

HELLO, WESLEY.

--YOU'RE TELLIN' ME THAT HIS ASS END HAS BEEN FLOATIN' AROUND DOWN IN THE SEWERS FOR *WEEKS?* AND WE ONLY JUST *NOW* FOUND HIM?

THE STATE OF DECOMPOSITION, THE DEGREE OF BLOOD LOSS, AND THE HYDROGENATION OF HIS TISSUES WOULD ALL SUGGEST SO, YES.

GIVEN THE LOCATION OF THE LOWER TRUNK, I'D SAY THAT THIS VICTIM, WHO- EVER HE WAS--

--FLOATED AROUND IN THE LARGER, MAIN CITY TUNNELS BEFORE EVENTUALLY CAUSING THE PLUG IN THIS TRIBUTARY.

LIKE ONE GIANT PIECE OF SHIT.

I'M TELLIN' YOU, HUBERT, EVERY DAY I THINK I'VE SEEN ALL THIS CITY HAS TO THROW OUT--

--AN' EVERY DAY I SEE SOME *NEW* REVOLTIN' DEVELOPMENT THAT MAKES ME WANNA PACK IT ALL IN.

I FULLY UNDERSTAND HOW YOU FEEL, LIEU- TENANT.

YEAH, I CAN SEE THAT.

Y'KNOW, THEY SPENT SIX HOURS LOOKIN' FOR THE OTHER HALF OF OUR HACKED- UP JOHN DOE AND DIDN'T FIND JACK--

--SHIT--

--NOT SO MUCH AS A FINGER FROM THIS GUY, MEANING SOME SICK BASTARD WALKED OFF WITH HIS TOP HALF AND THEN CHUCKED HIS--

HEY--!

-- WHAT THE HELL IS *THIS?*

DIAN?

I'M GLAD TO SEE YOU'RE GETTING OUT A BIT, WESLEY.

DIAN?

OR MAYBE THOSE WERE JUST THE JUVENILE CONCLUSIONS OF A BOY AT LOOSE IN AN EXOTIC LAND.

I--DIAN... I'D LOVE TO TALK TO YOU, REALLY--

THAT'S VERY... HEALTHY. I'D HATE TO THINK YOU WERE LOCKED IN YOUR HOME, MORIBUND OVER OUR TROUBLES.

DIAN? SHOULDN'T WE BE GETTING TO OUR TABLE?

UM... I'LL BE RIGHT WITH YOU, ELLA. I'D LIKE TO HEAR WHAT WESLEY HAS TO SAY AND THEN I'LL BE RIGHT OVER. OKAY?

ALL RIGHT... BUT DON'T BE LONG.

WELL?

DIAN...WHY-- WHY HAVE YOU BEEN AVOIDING ME?

AVOIDING YOU? WESLEY, I'VE JUST BEEN LIVING MY LIFE. YOU DIDN'T EXPECT ME TO SIMPLY STOP...

... DID YOU?

2

NIGHT OF THE BUTCHER

ACT · TWO

UH... OUT... YES--

I'VE BEEN THINKING LATELY OF HOW MUCH EASIER LOVE AND SEX APPEARED TO BE IN THE ORIENT.

NO, NO. BUT WE HAVEN'T EVEN TALKED SINCE--UH--

SINCE THAT NIGHT? NO WE HAVEN'T.

--BUT QUITE FRANKLY, I THINK I MADE MYSELF CLEAR WHEN I LEFT THAT EVENING.

BUT, DIAN--

THERE ARE DIFFERENCES BETWEEN US THAT SIMPLY CAN'T BE OVERLOOKED.

DIAN, PLEASE, I NEED TO EXPLAIN--

DIAN. THERE YOU ARE! COME ON, HONEY. SHOW'S ABOUT TO START. YOU DON'T WANNA MISS IT, DO YOU?

OF COURSE NOT, NICKY.

UH...

3

129

WHAT THE FUCK IS THIS!?

I'D SAY IT LOOKS LIKE A MICROPHONE. THOUGH SMALLER THAN ANY I'VE EVER SEEN.

A MICROPHONE?

A MICROPHONE!

YOU MEAN T'TELL ME THAT SOME CRANK'S BEEN LISTENIN' IN ON MY CONVERSATIONS?

YOU LISTENIN' T'ME NOW, YOU ASSHOLE? HUH?

YOU HEAR THE SOUND OF A MAN ABOUT TO KICK YOUR ASS SOON AS HE FINDS OUT WHERE THIS WIRE GOES?

WOOLSEY! BURKE.

I GOT A FUCKIN' MICROPHONE WIRE COMIN' OUT OF MY OFFICE AND GOIN' UP TO THE ROOF--

--AND YOU BETTER GET SOME MEN UP THERE TO STOP ME FROM KILLIN' WHOEVER IT IS.

HM...

4

WESLEY? I'D LIKE TO INTRODUCE MY... DATE, NICK AVANZINO.

DATE...?

PLEASURE T'MEETCHA.

WESLEY IS... AN OLD FRIEND.

UH...

THE SHOW'S STARTING. I--I'LL LET YOU GET BACK TO YOUR FRIEND. MAYBE WE CAN TALK LATER. GOOD EVENING.

...UH...

I THINK BACK ON MY TIME IN THE EAST AND I RECALL A DIFFERENT TYPE OF LOVE. IT WAS--

MAN, THAT'S TOUGH LUCK. AND JUST THE SORT OF SCENE I WAS SUPPOSED TO HELP YOU AVOID TONIGHT.

I TAKE IT THAT WAS SHE.

--SIMPLER.

UH, YES, YES, THAT WAS DIAN. I--OH, I DIDN'T INTRODUCE YOU, DID I? I'M SORRY, I DON'T KNOW WHERE MY HEAD--

SAY NO MORE, BROTHER. IT'S I WHO SHOULD BE APOLOGIZING.

BUT NOT UNTIL TOMORROW. OUR EVENING'S NOT SPOILED YET, AND CAN, IN FACT, ONLY GET BETTER FROM HERE ON.

YES...

...YES, I SUPPOSE YOU'RE RIGHT. CHEERS.

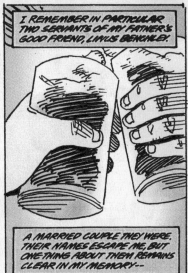

I REMEMBER IN PARTICULAR TWO SERVANTS OF MY FATHER'S GOOD FRIEND, LINUS BENGMLEY.

A MARRIED COUPLE THEY WERE. THEIR NAMES ESCAPE ME, BUT ONE THING ABOUT THEM REMAINS CLEAR IN MY MEMORY--

--THERE SEEMED TO BE NO TENSION BETWEEN THEM... EVER.

--A *TRANSMITTER?!* YOU MEAN T' TELL ME MY OFFICE'S BEEN TAGGED BY FRIGGIN' CAPTAIN RADIO AND THE AIR PIRATES?

I'LL TELL YOU *ONE* THING, MISTER--

--WHOEVER SET *THIS* BABY UP WAS PRETTY DARNED *CLEVER.*

TAPPED RIGHT INTO YOUR *OWN* RADIO FREQUENCIES HERE AT THE STATION.

SO LONG AS HE HAS THE ONLY RE-CEIVER, CHANCES ARE YOU'LL *NEVER* BE ABLE TO TRACE HIM.

GIMME THAT.

FUCK!

LIEUTENANT! WE COULDA CHECKED THAT FOR *PRINTS!*

YOU THINK WHOEVER DID THIS DIDN'T WEAR *GLOVES,* WOOLSEY?

YOU THINK HE WAS SMART ENOUGH TO BREAK INTO POLICE HEADQUARTERS, INSTALL A TRANS-MITTER MICROPHONE, CONCEAL SAID MICROPHONE, AND GET BACK OUT BUT TOO *STUPID* T' NOT WEAR GLOVES? HUH?!

NO.

DAMN RIGHT NO. HE AIN'T *STUPID*--

--BUT HE ALSO AIN'T *PERFECT.* HE'LL SCREW UP.

AN' WHEN HE DOES... *WHAM!* HIS NUTS ARE GONNA BE IN A VISE, AND MY HAND'S GONNA BE ON THE LOCKING LEVER.

6

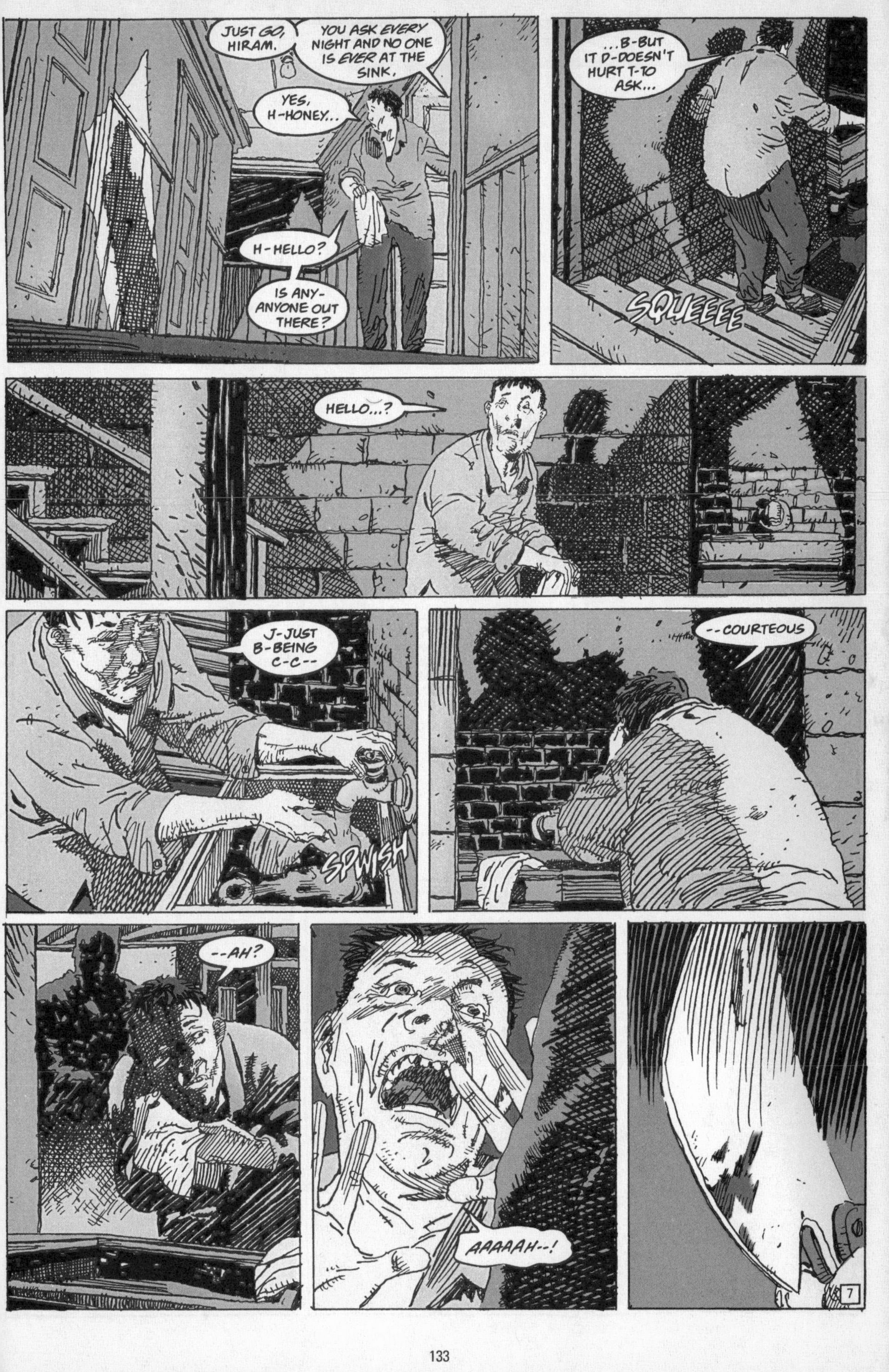
JUST GO, HIRAM.
YOU ASK EVERY NIGHT AND NO ONE IS EVER AT THE SINK.
YES, H-HONEY...
H-HELLO?
IS ANY-ANYONE OUT THERE?
...B-BUT IT D-DOESN'T HURT T-TO ASK...
SQUEEEE
HELLO...?
J-JUST B-BEING C-C--
SPWISH
--COURTEOUS
--AH?
AAAAAH--!
7

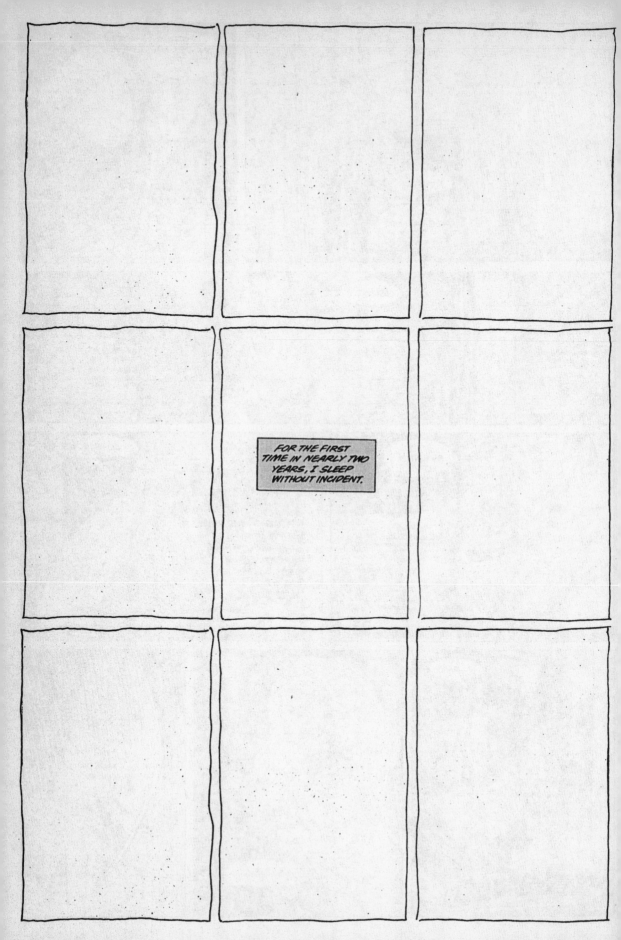

FOR THE FIRST TIME IN NEARLY TWO YEARS, I SLEEP WITHOUT INCIDENT.

OOHH... GOD...

BUT IN THE MORNING, I'M LEFT WITH TWO REMNANTS OF LAST NIGHT--

UNNNNH... HUMPHRIES...?

--A HANGOVER--

...HELP...

--AND MY THOUGHTS OF BENCHLEY'S SERVANTS.

THEY WERE SO ACCEPTING OF THEIR BOND TO ONE ANOTHER--

I'VE OFTEN FELT OUT OF STEP WITH THE REST OF THE WORLD FOR NOT HAVING A DRIVING PASSION FOR DRINK.

WHAT WAS I THINKING, HUMPHRIES?

I WOULD HAZARD TO GUESS YOU WERE TRYING NOT TO, SIR.

--AS IF THERE WAS AN UNWRITTEN CODE THAT STATED MEN AND WOMEN ARE TOGETHER--

I'VE PREPARED MY MOTHER'S FAVORITE MORNING-AFTER REMEDY--

SMELLS AWFUL.

--AND THAT IS ENOUGH.

OH, IT IS, BUT IT SAVED MUM AFTER MANY A BAWDY WEEKEND.

GAH! SHE DIDN'T HAVE AN IRON STOMACH BY ANY CHANCE--?

CAST-IRON, SIR.

9

I ALSO CAME ACROSS THIS LISTING IN THE CLASSIFIED COLUMNS.

GIVEN YOUR CONDITION, I DO HOPE YOU'LL DELAY ACTION UNTIL YOU'RE FULLY RECOVERED--

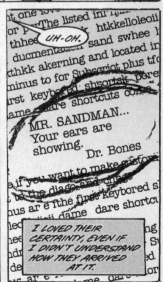

t one lov... or p The listed in... thhe htkkelloleoii sand swhee ducmentation kthkk akerning and located ir minus to for Subscript plus tfo rst keyboad shsortsk pore ame are shortcuts co

UH-OH.

MR. SANDMAN... Your ears are showing.

Dr. Bones

if you want to make... the diag... thus ar e the first keyboard s dame dare shortc

I LOVED THEIR CERTAINTY, EVEN IF I DIDN'T UNDERSTAND HOW THEY ARRIVED AT IT.

135

WITH BENCHLEY'S DOMESTICS, ONE NOT ONLY GOT THE FEELING THAT THEY ALWAYS WOULD BE TOGETHER--

--YOU LISTENIN' T'ME *NOW*, ASSHOLE? HUH?

--YOU HEAR THE SOUND OF A MAN ABOUT TO KICK YOUR ASS--

--BUT THAT THEY ALWAYS HAD BEEN TOGETHER. SPIRITUALLY.

DAMN IT.

--NO, I JUST WANT HIS *LIVER* KEPT ASIDE FOR SOME--

RING

JUST A MINUTE--

I HAVE RECEIVED AND UNDERSTOOD YOUR MESSAGE, HUBERT KLEIN.

OH YOU GOT IT, UH... *MOM*?

GOOD! I'M GLAD I COULD HELP. I JUST WANTED TO BE SURE YOU *KNEW*--

MR. KLEIN? THEY WANT YOU AT THIS CRIME SCENE RIGHT AWAY. 'NOTHER HATCHET JOB.

HARVEY? DOES THIS SAY 445 EAST 33RD--?

--I CAN'T QUITE READ IT--

I LONG FOR THAT EASE OF ENGAGE-MENT--

10

--EVEN IF I NO LONGER BELIEVE THAT I *DESERVE* IT.

--CAN'T *TELL* YOU HOW GLAD I AM TO SEE *THIS.* MAKES THE *PERFECT* ADDITION TO AN ALREADY *SWELL* WEEK.

LIEUTENANT? I JUST GOT THE MESSAGE. WE HAVE ANOTHER ONE ON OUR HANDS?

FAR AS I CAN TELL, BUT THAT'S WHY WE CALL *YOU,* HUBERT.

HAVE A LOOK-SEE WITH THOSE NEW SPECTACLES OF YOURS.

WELL... A SINGLE CLEAVING WOUND TO THE SKULL--STRANGE THOUGH--

--THERE DOESN'T SEEM TO BE ANYTHING *MISSING* FROM THIS CORPSE. SOME BRAIN MATTER, PERHAPS, BUT--

SPARE ME THE SMALL DETAILS--

I'D THINK THAT A VERY *IMPORTANT* DETAIL, LIEUTENANT. AFTER ALL, THE OTHERS WERE MISSING--

YEAH, I KNOW. NOT TO MENTION THE FACT THAT THEY WERE ALL HEFTS AND THIS GUY'S SKINNY AS A RAIL.

YOU KNOW, YOU'RE *RIGHT.* YOU... OY... YOU DON'T THINK THE KILLER COULD BE... *EATING* THESE--

YOU JUST KEEP THAT KIND OF SHIT TO YOURSELF, HUEY. LAST THING WE NEED'S WORD GETTIN' OUT THAT THERE'S SOME KIND OF *CANNIBAL* LOOSE IN THE CITY.

YOU! I NEED A HAND WITH SOMETHING DOWNSTAIRS. AND BY THE WAY--

--WHATEVER YOU JUST HEARD OF OUR CONVERSATION? YOU *DIDN'T* HEAR. GOT IT?

SURE.

11

WHAT EXACTLY WE LOOKIN' FOR, LIEUTENANT?

WE'RE LOOKIN' FOR AN *ENTRY*.

THE SUPER IN THIS SQUAT CLAIMS HE DIDN'T HEAR ANYONE COME IN THE *FRONT* WAY LAST NIGHT--

--SO, THAT LEAVES THE ROOF, THE BASEMENT, OR SOME WAY WE DON'T *KNOW* ABOUT.

ROOF'S TOO MUCH TROUBLE, AN' I ALREADY CHECKED THE BASEMENT, BUT SOME OF THESE OLD SHIT-SHACKS HAD--

UNH!

--*HERE* YA GO... HAD DRAINAGE PIPES OUTSIDE. *SEE?* THESE DUMPS NEVER HAD BASE-MENTS ORIGINALLY--

--SO I'M GUESSIN' WE'LL FIND A BOARDED-OVER DRAIN SOMEWHERE INSIDE THE BUILDING. GET A SEWER GUY OUT HERE TO LOOK INTO THIS TUNNEL, *PRONTO*.

PRETTY *SMART*, LIEUTENANT.

YEAH, THAT'S WHY I GET THE--

--GET THE--

12

--HEY!

WHAT?

GODDAMN!
CREEP!
ASSHOLE!

EASY, LIEUTENANT--

HE'S ALREADY GONE AND THERE'S PEOPLE'S *WINDOWS* UP THERE.

DON'T TOUCH MY FUCKIN' GUN!

YOU WANT I SHOULD PUT OUT AN *A.P.B.* ON 'IM?

NO, WHAT I WANT IS FOR YOU TO GET A GODDAMN *SEWER GUY* DOWN HERE AND IN THAT TUNNEL LIKE I TOLD YOU. *GOT IT?*

SURE.

THEN GET *MOVING.*

I'LL BE *INSIDE.*

13

OKAY, EVERYBODY, SAY "CLEAVER?"

WHAT--?

HM... WHAT WE HAVE HERE...?

WALLY? DID YOU GET A SHOT OF THIS MARK OUT IN THE HALL?

NAH, BUT I'VE GOT THE FILM IF YOU'VE GOT THE INCLINATION.

YES...PLEASE. I'M NOT SURE WHAT IT IS, BUT--

OH GOOD LORD! PHEW!

I GUESS I AM SURE WHAT IT IS, BUT I'D STILL LIKE A PHOTO TO PUT WITH THIS SAMPLE.

14

...SAME OLD THING...

...DAY IN, DAY OUT...

...WAKE UP, CHARLIE, YOU'RE LATE FOR WORK...

...ALL DAY LONG...

"...CHARLIE, HEAD UPTOWN WE GOT A CLOG..."

...CLIMB DOWN INTO THE SHIT...

WHO THE HELL YOU TALKIN' TO DOWN THERE?

...WALK AROUND IN THE SHIT...

...NEVER SHOULD'VE QUIT THOSE PIANO LESSONS--

NO ONE, OFFICER. NO ONE IMPORTANT LEASTWAYS.

WELL?

THERE'S DEFINITELY AN OLD DRAIN LINE HERE. LOOKS LIKE IT'S SEEN SOME FOOT TRAFFIC RECENTLY. GOT FRESH MUCK IN AN OTHERWISE DRY TUNNEL.

SO THIS COULD BE A REGULAR SUBWAY FOR A GUY IF HE KNEW WHERE HE WAS HEADIN'?

NAH. I MEAN, WE GET THE OCCASIONAL BUM CRAWLIN' IN TO GET OUT OF THE COLD. EVEN A LOST KID OR TWO--

-- BUT IT'S JUST TOO DAMN FOUL UNDERGROUND. NO ONE COULD SURVIVE THE FUMES DOWN THERE FOR LONG.

COUGH COUGH COUGH

YEAH, THOSE FUMES'LL KILL YA.

15

AN'-- (hic)-- AN' *THEN* HE SHESH... NOT IN *MY* WIFE'SH GIRDLE! HEH! HEH-HEH--

:BURP:

TELL ME WE'LL BE TOGETHER AGAIN SHOON?

OH, YOU NEVER KNOW, BRUNO. THAT *MIGHT* HAPPEN.

NO...UH...THAT'S ALL RIGHT. I HEAR THE *PHONE* RINGING, BUT THANKS ANYWAY. GOOD NIGHT.

SHALL I...COME IN?

RING RING

RING RING

HELLO, DIAN? IT'S WES. PLEASE DON'T HANG UP--

WES, I WOULDN'T HANG UP ON YOU. WHAT'S HAPPENING BETWEEN US ISN'T ABOUT TRYING TO HURT YOU.

I KNOW, I KNOW. I DIDN'T MEAN TO SUGGEST THAT, DIAN. I'M NOT CALLING BECAUSE I SAW YOU WITH THAT MAN THE OTHER NIGHT, I JUST--

--I NEED YOU, DIAN. MORE THAN I EVER REALIZED.

PLEASE DON'T DO THIS, WES. I'VE *TOLD* YOU THAT I NEED SOME TIME TO THINK ABOUT THIS. TO DECIDE WHAT I FEEL ABOUT ALL THAT'S HAPPENED--

FROM APPEARANCES I'D SAY YOU'VE ALREADY MADE *SOME* DECISIONS.

THAT'S NOT FAIR. I'M A YOUNG WOMAN, AND I DON'T PLAN TO SIMPLY STOP LIVING BECAUSE OF THIS. I'LL CALL YOU WHEN...

...AND *IF* I FEEL DIFFERENTLY, WESLEY.

UNTIL THEN, ALL I CAN SAY IS THAT I WISH YOU THE BEST, AND I PROMISE I WON'T TELL ANYONE WHAT I KNOW.

I--I UNDERSTAND, DIAN, AND I'M SORRY.

I'M JUST *SO* SORRY. GOOD... NIGHT...

FOR ALL MY RUMINATIONS ABOUT THE EAST AND THE WEST OF THE HEART--

--ALL I KNOW FOR CERTAIN--

16

--IS THAT AT THIS MOMENT, MINE IS DEFINITELY OF TWO WORLDS.

CLIK

=SIGH=

TONY--?

I DIDN'T THINK YOU WAS COMIN' BY TONIGHT.

YEAH, ME NEITHER, BUT I DIDN'T FEEL LIKE GOIN' HOME.

GOT AN UGLY CASE CHEWIN' ME UP.

SORRY TO HEAR IT. WHISKEY?

YEAH, GINA. THAT'D BE SWELL.

17

HERE YA GO, HANDSOME.

THANKS.

OOO, YOU *ARE* GRUMPY TONIGHT. ARE YOU SURE THERE ISN'T ANYTHING--

--ELSE I CAN DO FOR YOU?

NAH. TOO TENSE RIGHT NOW. LE/MME JUST SIT HERE AND SMOKE A BIT. THEN I'LL BE IN.

SUIT YOURSELF, SWEETIE.

THANKS, BABY.

TAK

18

FACELESS, OR WITHOUT TRUE FACE?

UNSCALABLE, OR WITHOUT ASCENDANT?

DESENSITIZED, OR WITHOUT SENSE?

HERE AT THE ONE WHO KNOWS YOU?

HERE WHERE ONE KNOWS ONESELF?

HERE WHERE SELF IS NOT KNOWN?

CRYING, OR WITHOUT REAL TEARS?

UNLOVED, OR WITHOUT HEART?

DISRESPECTED, OR WITHOUT HONOR?

19

'MORNING, CANELLA.

YOU TALKIN' TO *ME*...LIEUTENANT?

NO, IT'S JUST, *UH*...WELL, HERE'S THE UPDATES. ALSO, THE M.E. WANTS YOU TO CALL HIM AT HIS OFFICE. SAYS IT'S IMPORTANT.

SOMETHIN' THE *MATTER*?

ALWAYS *IS*.

ALWAYS IS.

HUEY? BURKE, WATTYA GOT FOR ME?

I'M GLAD YOU CALLED. I TOOK A SAMPLE FROM THE LAST SCENE. MY ANALYSIS SHOWS IT TO BE HUMAN WASTE MATERIALS COMBINED WITH TRACES OF OTHER SUBSTANCES--

--PETROLEUM OIL, TOBACCO ASH, UN-DIGESTED FOOD--

SO YOU FOUND SOME *SHIT* IN A FLOPHOUSE. WHAT'S THE BIG SURPRISE?

NOT JUST FECAL MATERIAL, LIEUTENANT. I WOULD POSTULATE THAT THE ONLY PLACE ONE WOULD FIND THIS ENTIRE MIXTURE IS IN A SEWER.

NOW *THAT'S* THE KINDA SHIT I *LIKE* TO HEAR ABOUT! CALL ME BACK LATER IF YOU GET ANYTHING ELSE.

LIEUTENANT! WE GOT ANOTHER ONE!

YEAH? I'M *READY*.

20

IT'S A SHEEP.

YEAH. THE FAMILY CAME HOME LAST NIGHT TO FIND SOMEONE HAD BUTCHERED IT.

IT'S A GODDAMN *SHEEP.* WHAT THE HELL'S IT DOIN' INSIDE AN *APARTMENT?*

SnFF

POLAKS, LIEUTENANT. YOU KNOW HOW FILTHY *THEY* CAN--

HOW'D THE SHEEP KILLER GET *IN* HERE?

FRONT DOOR WAS FORCED. THESE PLACES ARE MADE OF PAPER.

YOU CHECK THE *BASEMENT* YET?

BASEMENT? WHAT *FOR?*

FOOTPRINTS, MAYBE. BLOOD, MAYBE--

--A SEWAGE DRAIN *DEFINITELY.*

THUK

OH, *WHY?* WHY SOMEONE KILL OUR LITTLE NINA?

NINA--?

21

--WELL, LET ME HAVE YA TAKE A LOOK AT THIS *LIST*.

ANYTHING THESE ADDRESSES ALL HAVE IN *COMMON*? ANY CONNECTIONS OR PIPE DESTINATIONS? *ANYTHING*?

COMMON? YEAH. YOU'RE *STANDIN'* ON WHAT THEY ALL GOT IN COMMON, DICK. *THIS* DESTINATION.

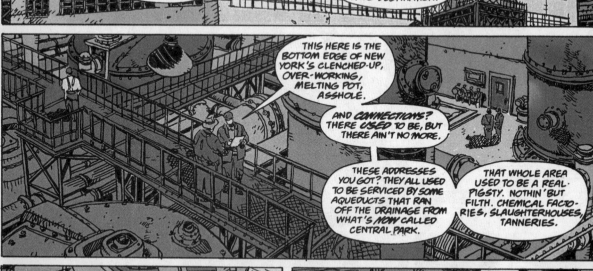

THIS HERE IS THE BOTTOM EDGE OF NEW YORK'S CLENCHED-UP, OVER-WORKING, MELTING POT, ASSHOLE.

AND *CONNECTIONS*? THERE *USED* TO BE, BUT THERE AIN'T NO MORE.

THESE ADDRESSES YOU GOT? THEY ALL USED TO BE SERVICED BY SOME AQUEDUCTS THAT RAN OFF THE DRAINAGE FROM WHAT'S *NOW* CALLED CENTRAL PARK.

THAT WHOLE AREA USED TO BE A REAL PIGSTY. NOTHIN' BUT FILTH. CHEMICAL FACTORIES, SLAUGHTERHOUSES, TANNERIES.

THOSE AQUEDUCTS STILL THERE?

NAH. WHEN THE CITY BUILT THE PARK, IT LAID IN A NEW SYSTEM. ALL THOSE OTHERS WERE SEALED OFF.

YOU GOT ANY CHARTS OF THIS OLD SYSTEM?

STOP! YOU SOME KINDA MORON, OR *WHAT*? YOU CAN'T LIGHT THAT THING IN HERE. METHANE'D SINGE YOUR MUSTACHE RIGHT OFF YOUR FACE.

ANSWER MY QUESTION.

YEAH, THERE'S CHARTS. HALL OF RECORDS'S GOT 'EM.

POPULAR *TOO*. YOU'RE THE *SECOND* GUY TO COME IN HERE ASKIN' ABOUT 'EM TODAY.

SECOND? WHO WAS THE OTHER ONE? WHAT'D HE LOOK LIKE?

WHO WAS HE? HOW SHOULD *I* KNOW? HE JUST LOOKED LIKE SOME GUY. HAT, COAT, GLASSES. MR. AVERAGE.

NOW IF I'M DONE KISSIN' YOUR ASS, MR. CITY OFFICIAL, I GOT A NEVER-ENDIN' JOB TO GET BACK TO.

22

I ASKED MY FATHER--

--YEARS LATER, AFTER WE'D LEFT HONG KONG--

--WHY IT WAS THAT BENCHLEY'S COUPLE SEEMED SO CONTENT WITH EACH OTHER--

23

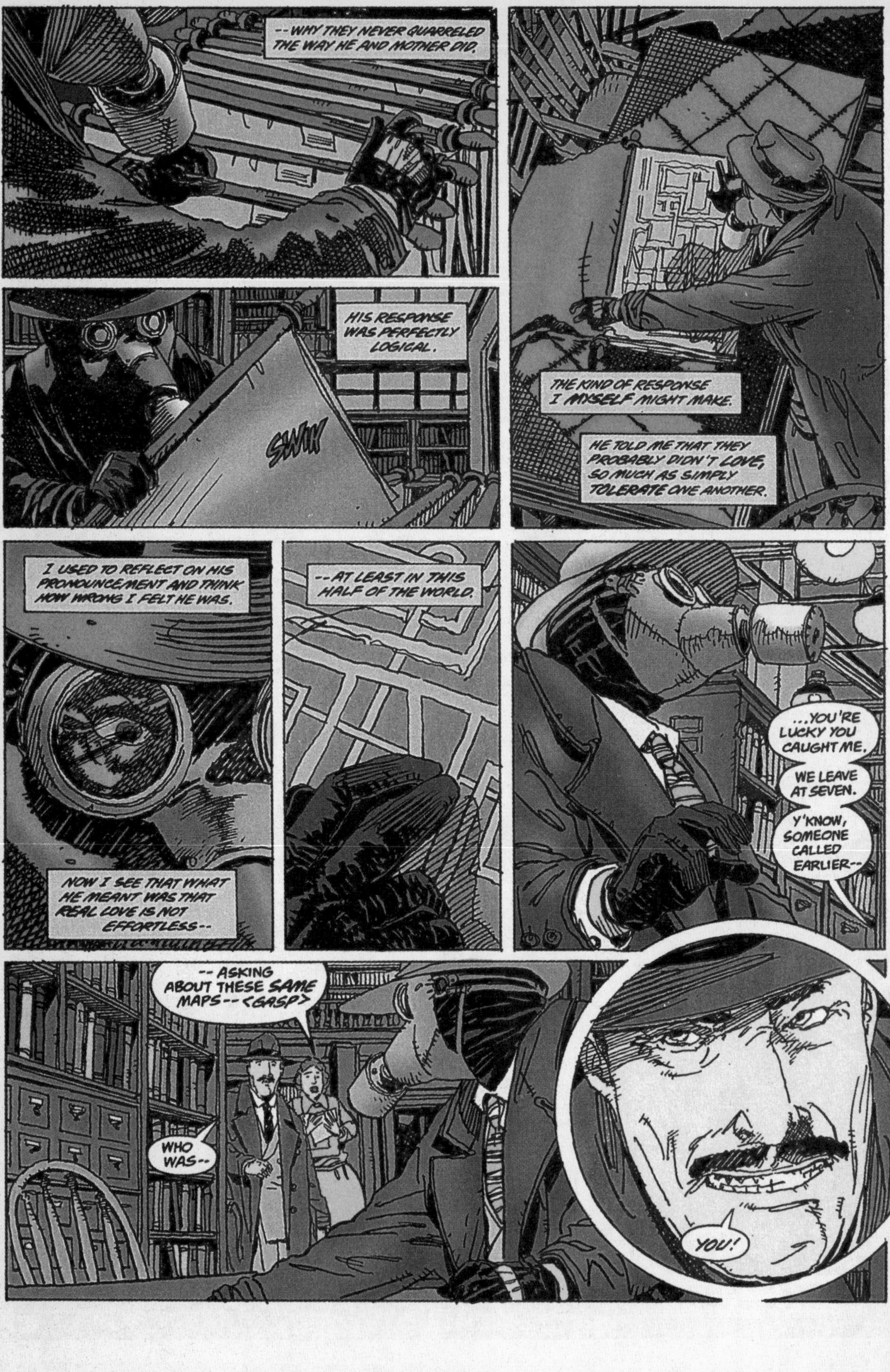
--WHY THEY NEVER QUARRELED THE WAY HE AND MOTHER DID.
HIS RESPONSE WAS PERFECTLY LOGICAL.
SWIK
THE KIND OF RESPONSE I MYSELF MIGHT MAKE.
HE TOLD ME THAT THEY PROBABLY DIDN'T LOVE, SO MUCH AS SIMPLY TOLERATE ONE ANOTHER.
I USED TO REFLECT ON HIS PRONOUNCEMENT AND THINK HOW WRONG I FELT HE WAS.
NOW I SEE THAT WHAT HE MEANT WAS THAT REAL LOVE IS NOT EFFORTLESS--
--AT LEAST IN THIS HALF OF THE WORLD.
...YOU'RE LUCKY YOU CAUGHT ME.
WE LEAVE AT SEVEN.
Y'KNOW, SOMEONE CALLED EARLIER--
--ASKING ABOUT THESE SAME MAPS-- <GASP>
WHO WAS--
YOU!

MY WORD!

YOU!

NOTHING GOOD COMES WITHOUT EFFORT.

I ONCE LAUGHED AT CLICHÉD TRUISMS OF THIS SORT, BUT NOW--

DON'T EVEN *THINK* IT, ASSHOLE! YOU'VE PULLED THAT STUNT ONE TOO MANY TIMES WITH ME!

AND I'LL TELL YOU SOMETHING ELSE, YOU *BEIN'* HERE TELLS ME WHO PUT THAT MICROPHONE IN MY OFFICE.

--IT SEEMS THE TRITE PHRASINGS OF CONTEMPORARY LIFE ARE SUDDENLY, INFURIATINGLY ACCURATE TO ME...

KRAACK

ONLY TIME I WANT SOMEONE LISTENIN' T'ME IS WHEN I'M *YELLIN'* AT 'EM! GOT IT?

...A CHILLING THOUGHT.

UNH--

OH *NO* YOU DON'T--

TAK-

151

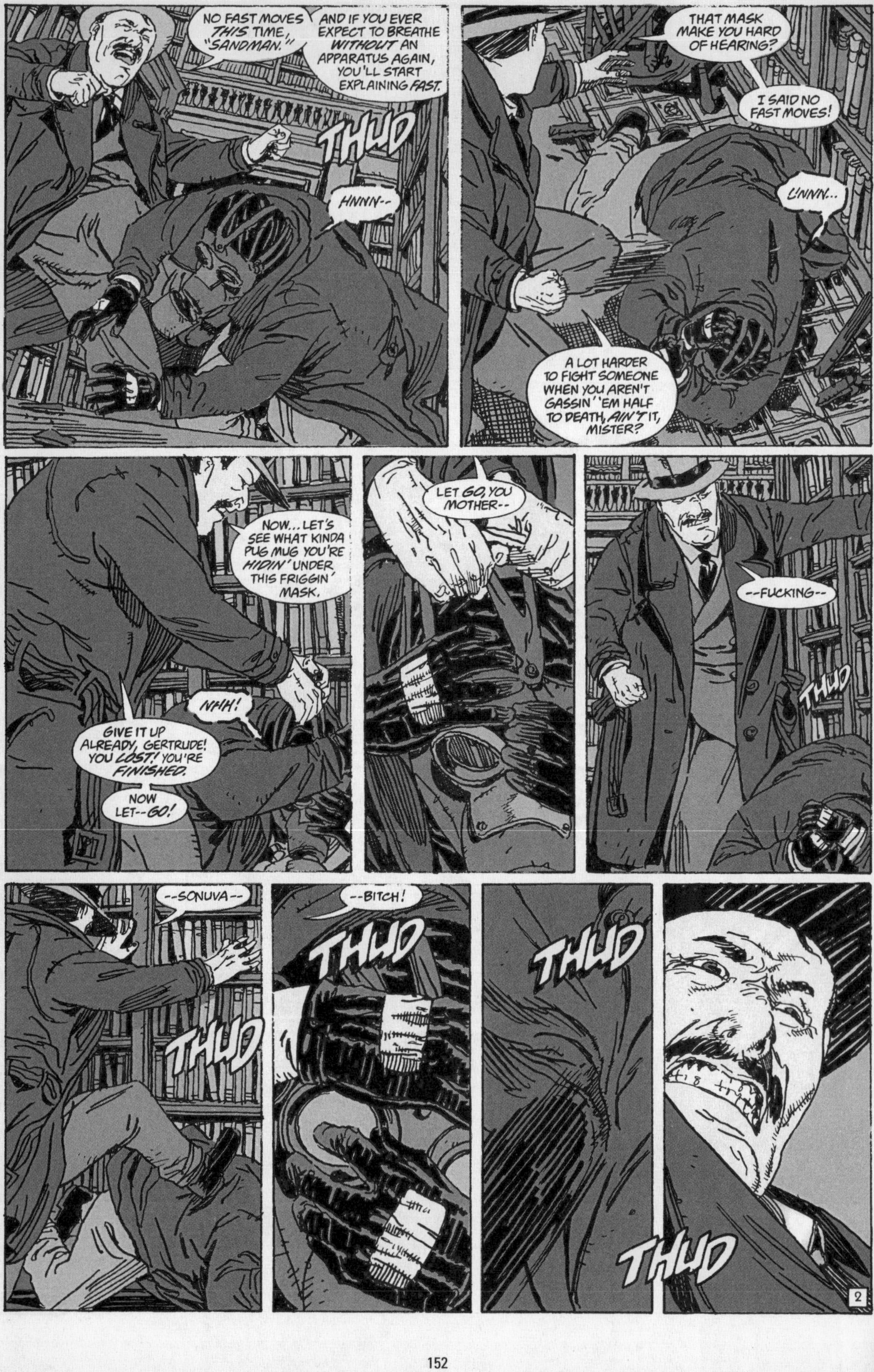
NO FAST MOVES THIS TIME, "SANDMAN."
AND IF YOU EVER EXPECT TO BREATHE WITHOUT AN APPARATUS AGAIN, YOU'LL START EXPLAINING FAST.
THUD
HNNN--
THAT MASK MAKE YOU HARD OF HEARING?
I SAID NO FAST MOVES!
UNNN...
A LOT HARDER TO FIGHT SOMEONE WHEN YOU AREN'T GASSIN' 'EM HALF TO DEATH, AIN'T IT, MISTER?
NOW... LET'S SEE WHAT KINDA PUG MUG YOU'RE HIDIN' UNDER THIS FRIGGIN' MASK.
NHH!
GIVE IT UP ALREADY, GERTRUDE! YOU LOST! YOU'RE FINISHED.
NOW LET--GO!
LET GO, YOU MOTHER--
--FUCKING--
THUD
--SONUVA--
THUD
--BITCH!
THUD
THUD
THUD
2

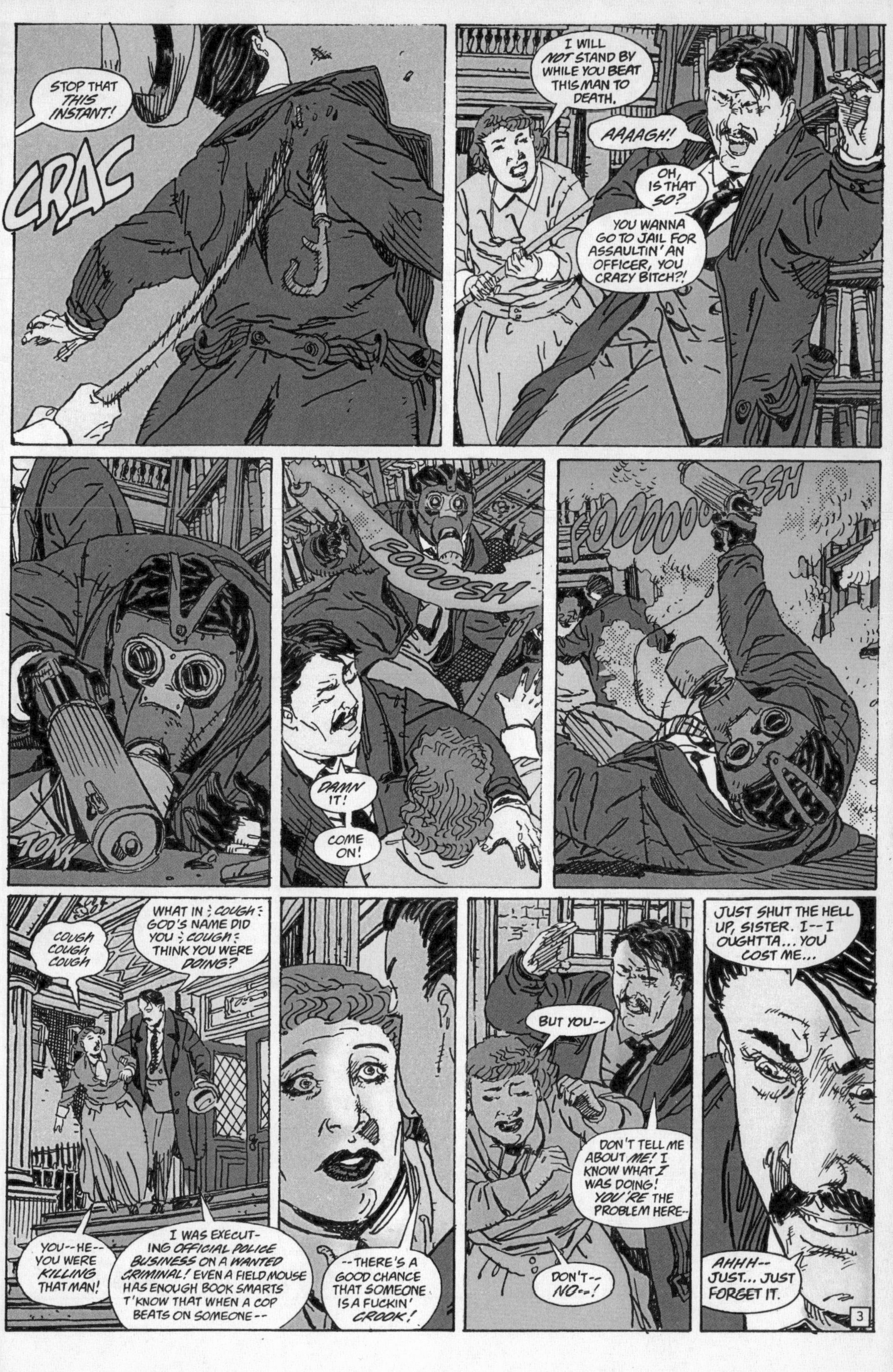
STOP THAT THIS INSTANT!
CRAC
I WILL NOT STAND BY WHILE YOU BEAT THIS MAN TO DEATH.
AAAAGH!
OH, IS THAT SO?
YOU WANNA GO TO JAIL FOR ASSAULTIN' AN OFFICER, YOU CRAZY BITCH?!
TOKK
FOOOSH
DAMN IT!
COME ON!
FOOOOOOSSH
COUGH COUGH COUGH
WHAT IN COUGH GOD'S NAME DID YOU COUGH THINK YOU WERE DOING?
YOU--HE-- YOU WERE KILLING THAT MAN!
I WAS EXECUTING OFFICIAL POLICE BUSINESS ON A WANTED CRIMINAL! EVEN A FIELD MOUSE HAS ENOUGH BOOK SMARTS T'KNOW THAT WHEN A COP BEATS ON SOMEONE--
--THERE'S A GOOD CHANCE THAT SOMEONE IS A FUCKIN' CROOK!
BUT YOU--
DON'T TELL ME ABOUT ME! I KNOW WHAT I WAS DOING! YOU'RE THE PROBLEM HERE--
DON'T-- NO--!
JUST SHUT THE HELL UP, SISTER. I-- I OUGHTTA... YOU COST ME...
AHHH-- JUST... JUST FORGET IT.
3

NIGHT OF THE BUTCHER
ACT · THREE

...THEN THE LITTLE BOY SAID, "BAH BAH BLACK SHEEP, HAVE YOU ANY WOOL?"

UH-OH, GEORGIE. MOMMY THINKS *YOU'VE* GOT A LITTLE BAG FULL TOO.

THAT'S ALL RIGHT THOUGH! YES IT IS! NO... DON'T YOU WORRY. MOMMY WILL CHANGE IT.

THAT'S WHAT MOMMIES ARE *FOR*, ISN'T IT? *ISN'T* IT, PUDDIN'?

YESSSS...

MY GOODNESS. I DON'T REMEMBER WHAT MOMMY FED YOU THIS MORNING, GEORGIE, BUT YOU DEFI-NITELY WON'T BE HAVING IT *AGAIN*.

4

"YES SIR, YES SIR, THREE BAGS FULL!" SAID THE SHEEP.

FOR THE LOVE OF ELEANOR WHAT'S...?

GEORGIE? PROMISE MOMMY THAT WHEN *YOU* GET TO BE A MAN YOU WON'T BE AS *FORGETFUL* AS DADDY.

THOUGH HOW ANYONE COULD FORGET TO FLUSH SO OFT--

WHAT IN THE *WORLD*--?...

OH, MY *GOD!*

5

ONE HORRIFYING THOUGHT IS THAT MY DESCENT INTO THE BANAL--

--MIGHT BE SOME SORT OF UNIVERSAL PAYBACK FOR PAST TRANSGRESSIONS.

CLANG

SEVERAL YEARS AGO I SAW A PRODUCTION OF A NEW WORK BY EUGENE O'NEILL--

UNNH!

--WHOSE NAME, INTERESTINGLY ENOUGH, DOES NOT ESCAPE ME--

--THOUGHT IT A TOUCHING, HEARTFELT, AND DEEPLY STIRRING DRAMA.

THUD

NNNNNNN--

--THE TITLE ESCAPES ME, BUT MY DATE, CONSTANCE--

"A PORTRAIT OF REAL LIVES AND REAL HEARTS," SHE REMARKED AFTERWARDS.

I CHUCKLED. AUDIBLY.

6

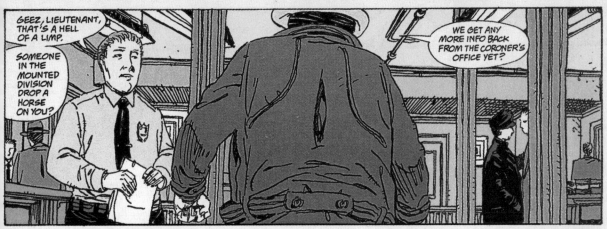

GEEZ, LIEUTENANT, THAT'S A HELL OF A LIMP.

SOMEONE IN THE MOUNTED DIVISION DROP A HORSE ON YOU?

WE GET ANY MORE INFO BACK FROM THE CORONER'S OFFICE YET?

NAH, NONE SO FAR. UH... YOU NEED A HAND OR SOMETHIN'?

YEAH, I'LL TAKE YOU UP ON THE "OR SOMETHING" AS LONG AS IT'S YOU GETTIN' THE HELL OFFA MY BACK FOR TWO SECONDS.

I'M JUST CONCERNED, SIR, YOU LOOK LIKE YOU'VE GOT A BREAK DOWN THERE.

BULLSHIT. IF MY FOOT WAS BROKEN, DO YOU THINK I'D STILL BE ABLE T'MOVE IT? NO, OF COURSE NOT.

WELL...

UNHH... SEE? JUST A FEW--

JESUS H. LIEUTENANT! WHAT THE HELL YOU'D DO TO IT?

I BRUISED IT KICKING A WALL. ALL RIGHT?

BUT--

AND DON'T EVEN THINK ABOUT ASKIN' ME WHY I WAS KICKIN' A WALL.

NOW WHAT D'YOU WANT?

OH YEAH, WELL, WE GOT ANOTHER ONE A' THEM BUTCHER JOBS.

SPILL IT.

SNOOTY BROAD UP ON 59TH FOUND A SHEEP'S HOOF IN HER CRAPPER.

WHY AM I NOT SURPRISED? COME ON.

7

--WATCHOO DOIN' DOWN THEAH, MISTUH BROWN TOE?

SAY WATCHOO DOIN'? YOU *DEAD*?

WATCHOO--

DON'T LIKE NO DEAD 'NS.

NO SIR, FOUND ONE DEAD 'N LAST WEEK. WASTED HISSELF AWAY THAT 'N DID.

WELL...IF 'N YOU *IS* DEAD, YOU AIN'T GONNA BE NEEDIN' NONE A' YO' PERSONALS.

BUT *ME*, SIR? ONLY LUCK FOUND *ME* LATELY'S BEEN *BAD*.

THIS HEAH DONE CHANGE THAT, THOUGH.

NOW LET'S SEE ABOUT THET COAT O' YOURS. LOOKS A MIGHT MORE STURDY THAN--

MARY MAGDELENE!

YOU A--A--WAR VET?

8

DON'T LIKE TAKIN' FROM A VET'RAN, NO SIR.

DON' NEED NO MASK THOUGH. THET WAR'S DONE OVUH WITH.

...UNHHH...

I BE DAMNED! YOU STILL *ALIVE!*

...WHAT? WHO--WHO ARE--MY *MASK!*

NO! DON'T LOOK AT ME! KEEP AWAY--

NO DON'T! I'LL GIVE IT ALL BACK--

I--

SHINP

I--

FOOOSH

MY PRONOUNCEMENT ABOUT O'NEILL'S PLAY UNINTENTIONALLY DROVE CONSTANCE AWAY FROM ME.

>COUGH<

IT WAS A FAST AND DECISIVE SEVERANCE THAT I WOULD NEVER HAVE EXPECTED.

I OFTEN WONDERED WHAT MIGHT HAVE BECOME OF US AS A COUPLE HAD I KEPT MY FEELING FROM HER IN THAT ONE CRITICAL MOMENT.

I REMEMBER TELLING MYSELF TO *LEARN* FROM THAT EXPERIENCE.

BUT MY PRESENT SITUATION SHOWS ME HOW LITTLE I STILL UNDERSTAND.

9

...YOU HEARD ME, *BOY SCOUTS.* YOU KNOW, GOD AND COUNTRY, CAMPING, TYING KNOTS, BUILDING LEAN-TOS?

YEAH, YEAH, I *KNOW* WHAT IT IS, BUT I DON'T KNOW WHY YOU WANNA KNOW IF I WAS ONE.

FACT IS, FRANCINE, I'VE GOT ENOUGH RANKS UP ON YOU THAT YOU DON'T *ASK* ME QUESTIONS, YOU JUST *ANSWER* MINE.

THAT'S *FRANCIS,* LIEUTENANT. MY MA WOULD BE MIGHTY UPSET IF SHE HEARD YOU CALL ME--

FRANCINE, THE BOY SCOUTS TEACHES A KID A LOT ABOUT BEIN' A GOOD MAN, BUT IT ALSO TEACHES A COP HOW T' BE A GOOD *DETECTIVE.*

LIKE ME, I GOT *MY* FIRST REAL BADGE IN NAVIGATION.

YOU?

NOW, YOU TAKE YOUR AVERAGE JOE, SAY *YOU,* FRANNY--

--HE GETS A COMPLEX SET OF DIAGRAMS LIKE THESE OLD SEWER CHARTS AND HE'S JUST UP SHIT CREEK.

WELL....

ME ON THE OTHER HAND, WITH THE KNOWLEDGE OF THE SCOUTS BEHIND ME, I CAN TRACE THIS THING LIKE IT WAS YESTERDAY'S NEWS.

UH-HUH. LOOK HERE. SHEEP LADY'S HOUSE SITS RIGHT IN THIS AREA *HERE,* WHERE NUMBER 7 OF THE CENTRAL DUCTS USED TO RUN.

BET YA EVEN MONEY THAT SOME OF THESE LINES ARE STILL *OPEN* SOMEHOW.

HOW WOULD WE FIND THAT OUT FOR SURE?

MUCH AS I HATE TO SAY IT, WE'D HAVE TO GO DOWN IN THERE.

10

ABSOLUTELY *NOT.* THE SECRETARY'S OUT UNTIL--

SECRETARY?! LOOK, LARRY, I'M ON THIS FUCKER'S TAIL. I CAN *FEEL* IT.

I NEED THAT WARRANT *NOW.* I'M ONLY TALKIN' ABOUT FIVE LOCATIONS HERE IN THE MID-TOWN AREA.

FIVE? YOU WANT TO GO DIGGING IN *FIVE* MID TOWN ESTABLISHMENTS? WHAT IN THE DEVIL DO YOU NEED THAT *MANY* FOR? ONE IS GOING TO BE DIFFICULT ENOUGH TO--

LOOK, IT'S NOT LIKE SURGERY HERE. I'VE NARROWED IT DOWN TO WHAT LOOK TO BE THE FEW EASIEST ACCESS POINTS TO THAT OLD SYSTEM. NOT *MY* FAULT THEY'RE ALL ALONG BASEMENTS OF SOME RESTAU-RANTS AND HOUSES.

THAT'S NOT GOING TO MAKE US VERY POPULAR WITH THOSE TENANTS AND RESIDENTS.

YOU LOOKIN' TO WIN A POPULARITY CONTEST OR YOU LOOKIN' TO STOP A SICK BASTARD WHO'S CUTTIN' UP THOSE SELF-SAME RESIDENTS?

SOMETHIN' ELSE I AIN'T TOLD YA YET TOO. THE *M.E.* THINKS THIS SICK-O MAY BE *EATIN'* PARTS OF THESE VICTIMS.

YOU'RE JOKING...YOU'RE *NOT* JOKING?

VERY WELL, LIEUTENANT. I'LL TALK TO JUDGE BAKKEN WHEN HE GETS BACK FROM THE DELI.

THANKS. ENJOY YOUR LUNCH.

11

ROMANTIC ENTANGLEMENTS ARE SO DAMN UNPREDICTABLE.

IN THAT CASE THE TRUTH SEVERED ALL TIES I SHARED WITH CONSTANCE.

AND YET, CONCEALING THE TRUTH HAS RESULTED IN MY CURRENT PREDICAMENT WITH DIAN.

AND NATURALLY, AS IF I DON'T FEEL BAD ENOUGH AS IT IS --

CLIK

-- IT SUDDENLY OCCURS TO ME THAT THESE ARE THE VERY ISSUES THE CHARACTERS IN THE O'NEILL PLAY WERE CONFRONTING --

-- THE TENUOUS NATURE OF THEIR FEELINGS FOR ONE ANOTHER --

-- THE RECKLESS WAYS IN WHICH THEY EXPRESSED THOSE FEELINGS --

12

--AT ONE MOMENT, RUSHING HEADLONG TOWARD DISASTER BECAUSE THEY WERE UNABLE TO GAIN CONTROL OVER THEM-SELVES--

--AND THE NEXT, FEELING SPENT FOR THEIR EXPRESSION--

--RECOILING FROM THE EXPLOSIONS OF PASSION THEY COULD NOT CONTAIN--

WOANG

CHUNGG

--LEFT AT AN UNEASY, YET UNAVOIDABLE EQUILIBRIUM.

THEIR ENTIRE BEINGS DAMAGED BY THE FICKLE WORKINGS OF ONE SMALL MUSCLE IN THEIR CHESTS.

MELODRAMA.

NUMBER SIX? WHAT ON EARTH HAVE YOU GOTTEN INTO...?

13

...A TRAMP? YOU'RE LUCKY YOU MADE IT BACK WITH YOUR *GLASSES*, SIR. THERE ARE STILL SOME DESPERATE FELLOWS LIVING IN THE AVENUES.

YES, THAT'S TRUE. IT'S NOT THE MONEY THAT'S GOT ME TROUBLED, THOUGH, HUMPHRIES.

NO?

BECAUSE OF THE STITCHING I TOOK FROM *BURKE*, WHEN I BROKE TO THE ALLEY, I COLLAPSED.

BUT WHEN I CAME TO, THIS HOBO REMOVED MY *MASK*. HE SAW MY *FACE*, HE--

I WOULDN'T WORRY OVER IT *TOO* MUCH, SIR. HE PROBABLY HAD DRUNK AWAY ANY MEMORY OF YOU BY NOW.

YES, I SUPPOSE THAT'S *TRUE*, BUT STILL, AFTER SO MANY MONTHS OF SECRECY, IT'S AS IF *EVERYONE* IS FINDING--

--OW!

PAIN?

YES!

THAT'S NOT GOOD. I'M AFRAID YOU MAY HAVE CRACKED A RIB.

WELL?

UNFORTUNATELY, THIS IS MORE THAN *I* CAN TEND TO. WE MAY HAVE TO SUMMON DR. McNIDER.

DAMN... HE'S A NOSY ONE *TOO*.

IT'S EITHER THAT OR--

NO, NO. CALL HIM. BUT AT LEAST GIVE ME SOME OF THOSE PAIN TABLETS BEFORE--

I WONDERED WHY NO ONE ANSWERED THE DOOR--

14

--I SHOULD HAVE KNOWN IT WAS JUST BUSINESS AS USUAL HERE AT THE DREAM FACTORY.

...DIAN...

MELODRAMA.

WHAT HAPPENED, WES? WERE YOU PLAYING CATCH WITH THE SIDEWALK AGAIN?

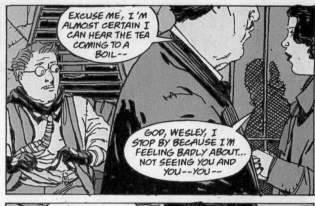

EXCUSE ME, I'M ALMOST CERTAIN I CAN HEAR THE TEA COMING TO A BOIL--

GOD, WESLEY, I STOP BY BECAUSE I'M FEELING BADLY ABOUT... NOT SEEING YOU AND YOU--YOU--

--NOTHING HAS CHANGED WITH YOU.

I THOUGHT MY DECISION MIGHT AT LEAST GIVE YOU PAUSE--

THERE IS NO PAUSE FROM WHAT I SEE, WHAT I MUST DO.

NOT EVEN FOR ME?

AS LONG AS YOU WALK THE CITY IN WHICH THESE MONSTERS DO THEIR BUSINESS, I CAN'T IGNORE IT.

BESIDES, THIS ISN'T AS BAD AS IT LOOKS, REALLY.

IS THAT SO? WES, I SAW THE BANDAGES.

IT'S JUST... THE TRUTH IS, I HAVEN'T BEEN FUNCTIONING WELL WITHOUT YOU, DIAN. THE DREAMS...THEY ONLY CONFUSE ME NOW. I'M LOST WITHOUT--

PLEASE DON'T SAY IT.

I DON'T LIKE THIS, WES. NOT ONE BIT. I'VE...GOT TO GO--

YES. OF COURSE. YOU SHOW UP UNANNOUNCED AND EXPECT SOME PICTURE PERFECT SCENARIO OVER NIGHT? I THOUGHT MORE OF YOU, DIAN.

IS THAT ALL YOU CAN MANAGE BY WAY OF SWEET TALK?

DAMN IT, DIAN! THERE IS SOMEONE OUT THERE IN THAT CONCRETE AND IRON JUNGLE THIS VERY INSTANT WHO IS HACKING INNOCENT SOULS TO DEATH.

I'VE GOT TO GO--

YOU CAN'T EXPECT ME TO JUST IGNORE THAT FACT.

I...I DON'T KNOW...WHAT I EXPECT.

MELODRAMA WHICH SEEMS TO REFLECT MY OWN LIFE MORE AND MORE WITH EACH PASSING MOMENT.

LIEUTENANT! THIS IS HARDLY GIVIN' AT ALL. SHOULD WE CHALK THIS ONE UP WITH THE FIRST? I DON'T THINK THERE'S NOTHIN' HERE.

I'LL DO THE *THINKING*, YOU JUST KEEP DIGGING!

ALL RIGHT, BUT--

TRUST ME, IT'S JUST A MATTER OF TIME. THOSE TUNNELS RAN RIGHT THROUGH HERE. NO WAY WE AREN'T GOING TO--

BRRT BRRT BRRT

WAIT A MINUTE!

FEELS LIKE I GOT SOMETHIN' MIGHTY HARD HERE.

TOK

YEAH? WELL I GOT SOMETHIN' HARD HERE FOR YOU IF IT AIN'T MY *GODDAMN* TUNNEL.

JUST WORK AT IT A LITTLE WITH THE--

CHOK CHOK

NOPE...NOPE, SORRY. LOOKS LIKE THIS ONE'S SEAL IS STILL INTACT TOO.

YEAH, IT'S COMPLETELY FILLED IN. NO ONE'S BEEN IN *OR* OUT FROM HERE.

SHIT.

AH WELL, LET'S MOVE ON TO THE NEXT LOCATION.

MAYBE THE THIRD TIME'LL BE THE CHARM.

16

166

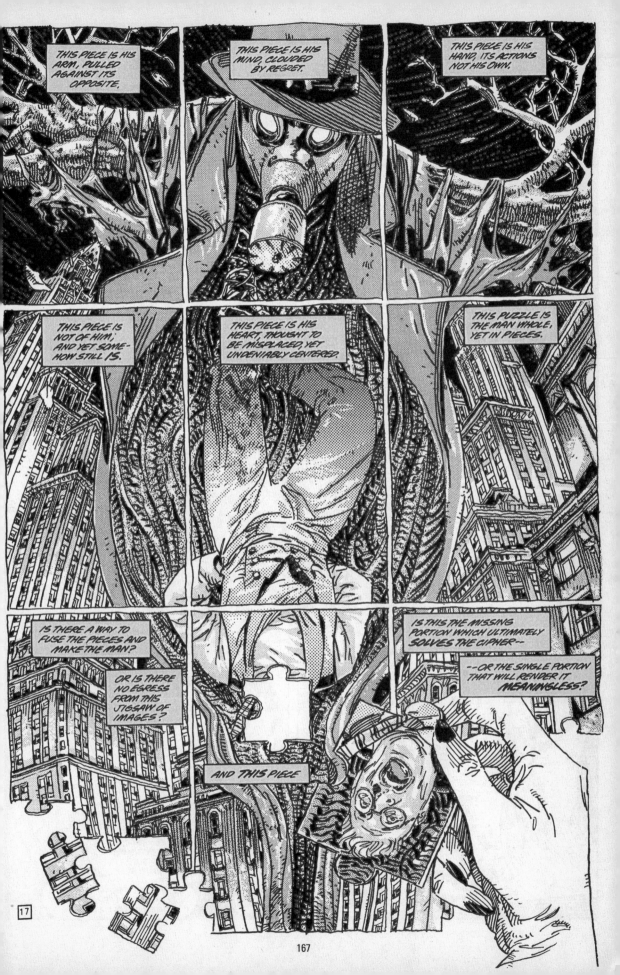

THIS PIECE IS HIS ARM, PULLED AGAINST ITS OPPOSITE.

THIS PIECE IS HIS MIND, CLOUDED BY REGRET.

THIS PIECE IS HIS HAND, ITS ACTIONS NOT HIS OWN.

THIS PIECE IS NOT OF HIM, AND YET SOME-HOW STILL IS.

THIS PIECE IS HIS HEART, THOUGHT TO BE MISPLACED, YET UNDENIABLY CENTERED.

THIS PUZZLE IS THE MAN WHOLE, YET IN PIECES.

IS THERE A WAY TO FUSE THE PIECES AND MAKE THE MAN?

OR IS THERE NO EGRESS FROM THIS JIGSAW OF IMAGES?

IS THIS THE MISSING PORTION WHICH ULTIMATELY SOLVES THE CIPHER--

--OR THE SINGLE PORTION THAT WILL RENDER IT MEANINGLESS?

AND THIS PIECE

17

167

--NO. I SIMPLY CAN *NOT* ALLOW THIS. ABSOLUTELY *NOT*.

GET THIS THROUGH YOUR THICK SKULL, FRENCHY. IT WASN'T A *REQUEST*, IT WAS A *STATEMENT*. WE'RE DIGGING UP YOUR WINE CELLAR.

BUT THIS IS OUR LUNCH HOUR! IT'S AN EXTREMELY *IMPORTANT* DAY FOR US. THE *MAYOR* IS DINING HERE.

YEAH? TELL HIM I NEED A RAISE WHEN YOU SEE 'M.

MEANTIME, GET YOUR ASS OUT OF THE WAY, 'CAUSE I'VE GOT A *WARRANT* HERE THAT SAYS WE'RE DIGGING.

WHAT YOU ASK IS...IS... *IMPOSSIBLE!*

I AIN'T *ASKIN'!* GOT IT!?

THIS IS *ABSURD*. I *DEMAND* YOUR BADGE NUMBER. THERE *WILL* BE A COMPLAINT FILED!

HMM... WHAT YA GOT COOKIN' HERE? SMELLS A LITTLE ...*ODD*--

OH...THAT, THAT IS OUR SPECIALTY, A LIGHT--

--COURSE I'M NO *GOURMET* OR ANYTHING, BUT I'D SAY IT'S SPOILED--

SPASSSH

WHAT HAVE YOU DONE?

I--THAT-- I--I'LL HAVE YOU *ARRESTED* FOR THAT!

ARREST A COP? DON'T MAKE ME LAUGH.

AND A SPILLED POT'S NOT EVEN THE *HALF* OF WHAT YOU'RE GONNA GET IF YOU DON'T QUIT FUCKIN' WITH ME.

NOW POINT THE WAY TO THAT CELLAR, YOU LITTLE TOAD. AND I MEAN *NOW*.

18

THAT NOISE IS *DEAFENING!*

IS THERE A PARROT DOWN HERE? I COULD SWEAR I'M STILL HEARIN' TALKIN' WHERE THERE SHOULDN'T *BE* ANY.

HEY, HEY! WE GOT A BREAK-THROUGH HERE.

YEAH? BACK AWAY AND LET ME GET A LOOK.

BRRRT BRRRT BRRRT

JUST A MINUTE, LIEUTENANT. I THINK I CAN GET THAT OPENED UP A BIT MORE FOR YA. GIVE YA A BETTER--

CHOF

PHEW! CHRIST ALMIGHTY WHATTA STENCH!

WHAT *IS* IT?

TAKE MY WORD FOR IT, NOTHIN' YOU'D WANNA TAKE HOME TO THE MISSUS.

YEP, JUST WHAT I FIGGERED ...PAY DIRT.

CLICK

I WANNA SEE WHAT'S IN THIS GODFOR-SAKEN SHIT HOLE...

FRANCIS? PAY OFF THE WORKMEN. WE'RE DONE WITH THEM. GO GET ME THE ROPE LADDER AND THOSE MINING HELMETS OUTTA THE CAR.

RIGHT AWAY, SIR.

19

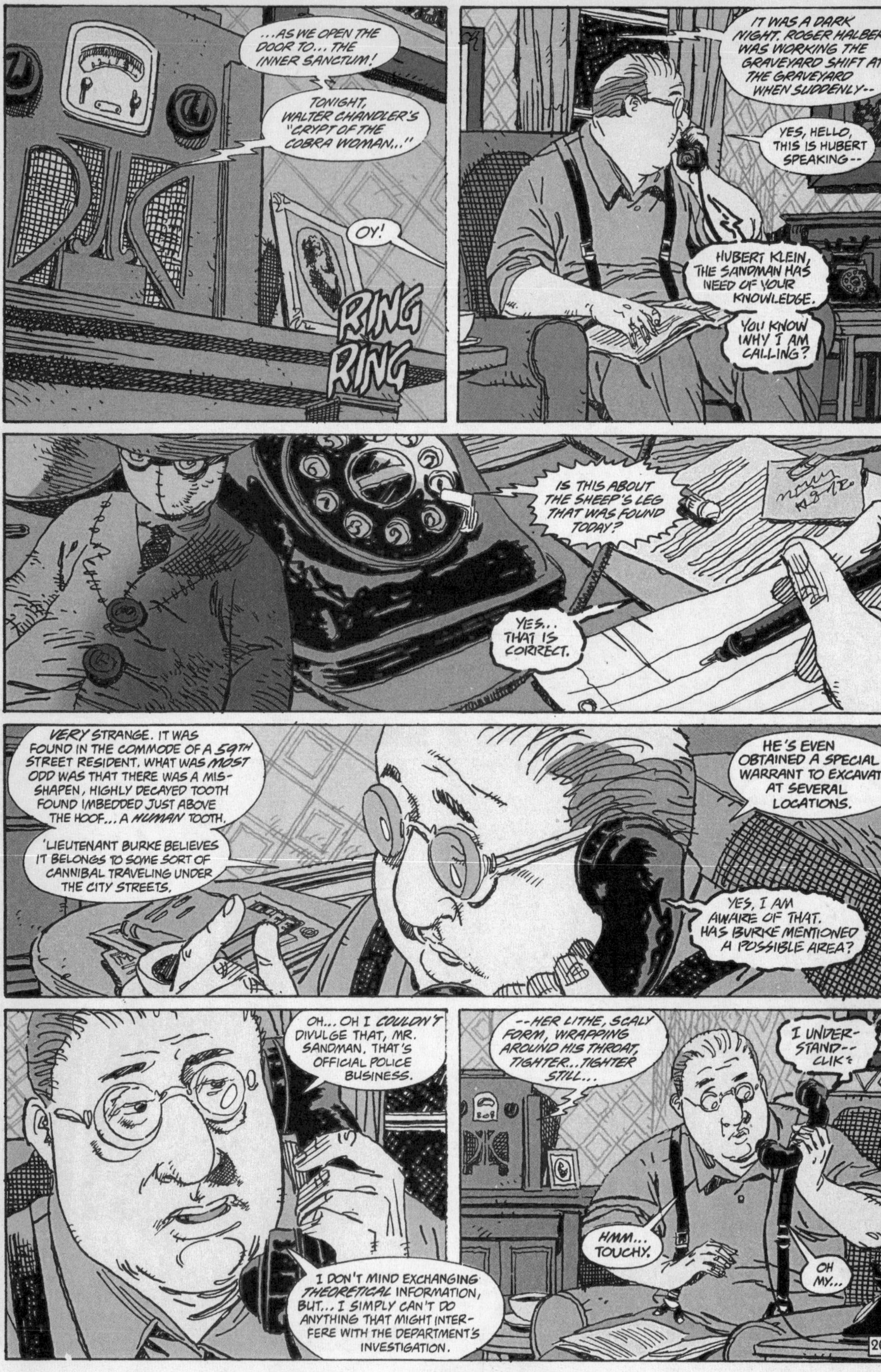
...AS WE OPEN THE DOOR TO... THE INNER SANCTUM!
TONIGHT, WALTER CHANDLER'S "CRYPT OF THE COBRA WOMAN..."
OY!
RING RING
IT WAS A DARK NIGHT. ROGER HALBERT WAS WORKING THE GRAVEYARD SHIFT AT THE GRAVEYARD WHEN SUDDENLY--
YES, HELLO, THIS IS HUBERT SPEAKING--
HUBERT KLEIN, THE SANDMAN HAS NEED OF YOUR KNOWLEDGE.
YOU KNOW WHY I AM CALLING?
IS THIS ABOUT THE SHEEP'S LEG THAT WAS FOUND TODAY?
YES... THAT IS CORRECT.
VERY STRANGE. IT WAS FOUND IN THE COMMODE OF A 59TH STREET RESIDENT. WHAT WAS MOST ODD WAS THAT THERE WAS A MIS-SHAPEN, HIGHLY DECAYED TOOTH FOUND IMBEDDED JUST ABOVE THE HOOF... A HUMAN TOOTH.
'LIEUTENANT BURKE BELIEVES IT BELONGS TO SOME SORT OF CANNIBAL TRAVELING UNDER THE CITY STREETS.
HE'S EVEN OBTAINED A SPECIAL WARRANT TO EXCAVATE AT SEVERAL LOCATIONS.
YES, I AM AWARE OF THAT. HAS BURKE MENTIONED A POSSIBLE AREA?
OH... OH I COULDN'T DIVULGE THAT, MR. SANDMAN. THAT'S OFFICIAL POLICE BUSINESS.
I DON'T MIND EXCHANGING THEORETICAL INFORMATION, BUT... I SIMPLY CAN'T DO ANYTHING THAT MIGHT INTER-FERE WITH THE DEPARTMENT'S INVESTIGATION.
--HER LITHE, SCALY FORM, WRAPPING AROUND HIS THROAT, TIGHTER... TIGHTER STILL...
I UNDER-STAND--
CLIK
HMM... TOUCHY.
OH MY...
20

PHEW

GOSH, IT SURE IS *RIPE* DOWN HERE.

YEAH, BUT I'M NOT CONVINCED IT'S AS BAD AS THE SMELL COMIN' OUT OF THAT KITCHEN UPSTAIRS. I COULD SWEAR I SAW THAT COOK PUTTIN' RAT *TURDS* IN SOMETHIN'.

CAPERS.

CAPERS? I THINK HACKIN' PEOPLE TO DEATH QUALIFIES AS FULL-BLOWN *CRIMES.*

NO, THAT'S WHAT HE WAS--

YOU TWO, PIPE DOWN. YOUR RATTLING'S GIVING ME A HEADACHE.

WHAT ARE WE LOOKING FOR EXACTLY?

ANYTHING SUSPECT--

--LIKE, SAY, A SHACK IN THE MIDDLE OF AN ABANDONED SEWER TUNNEL F'RINSTANCE.

YOU THINK A *PERSON* BUILT THAT? *HERE?*

WELL, IF IT WASN'T A PERSON, THERE'S SOME PRETTY FUCKIN' INGENIOUS RATS LIVING DOWN HERE. LET'S GET A CLOSER LOOK.

LOOK AT ALL THAT CRAP. SOMEBODY'S LIVIN' DOWN HERE, LIKE I BEEN SAYIN' ALL ALONG.

I DON'T KNOW, LIEUTENANT. LOOKS TO BE LONG *GONE* TO ME. MAYBE SOME DEPRESSION FLOP--

UN-UH. LOOK HERE.

HOLY SHIT, YOU THINK SOMEONE HAD *KIDS* LIVIN' WITH 'EM DOWN HERE?

IF SO, I'D HATE TO SEE 'EM NOW. I DON'T SEE HOW ANYONE COULD TAKE THIS SMELL FOR LONG.

COME ON, LET'S KEEP MOVIN'.

21

LITTLE DID I REALIZE AS I STRUGGLED THROUGH THE PLAY WITH CONSTANCE--

-- THAT O'NEILL ACTUALLY UNDERSTOOD FAR MORE THAN I GAVE HIM CREDIT FOR.

I READ LATER, IN THE TRIBUNE I BELIEVE, THAT O'NEILL FELT THAT MAN'S ONLY HOPE OF LIVING A FULFILLING LIFE--

YES, HELLO?

HELLO, WESLEY.

DIAN, I'M GLAD YOU CALLED. I'M SORRY I SNAPPED AT YOU EARLIER. I WAS JUST...WELL, I LOST MY HEAD.

-- WAS STRIVING FOR THE UN-ATTAINABLE.

ACTUALLY, I CALLED ABOUT THE CASE. THE KILLINGS YOU MENTIONED? I SUPPOSE YOU'VE HEARD LT. BURKE'S THEORY THAT THE KILLER LIVES IN THE SEWERS...

ONLY THE MOST IMPOSSIBLE OF LOVES--

-- WAS TRULY WORTH A MAN'S DEVOTION TO IT.

YES, I HAVE, UNFORTUNATELY, THAT LITTLE BIT OF INFORMATION LEAVES AN AWFUL LOT OF AREA TO INVESTIGATE. BURKE APPARENTLY HAS A LEAD, I ONLY WISH I KNEW WHERE HE--

I KNOW WHERE HE'S LOOKING.

THIS MADE ME REALIZE IT WASN'T MELODRAMA I HAD SEEN ON STAGE--

HE FOUND SOMETHING IN THE BASEMENT OF BLANCO NEGRO, THAT FRENCH RESTAURANT OVER IN--

WHERE DID YOU--

I HAVE MY SOURCES. WELL... A SOURCE. NAME OF LARRY. CHARMING CHAP. YOU'D LIKE HIM.

I APPRECIATE THIS, DIAN... BUT WHY ARE YOU HELPING ME. YOU KNOW I'LL USE THIS TO--

I DO KNOW, BUT I ALSO KNOW I'VE NOT BEEN ABLE TO STOP THINKING ABOUT YOU, THINKING ABOUT WHAT IT IS YOU DO.

AND THOUGH I MAY NOT UNDER-STAND WHY,...YET,... I JUST FEEL THAT I CAN'T IGNORE THESE SITUATIONS EITHER.

--IT WAS A PORTRAIT OF REAL LIVES-- AND REAL HEARTS.

22

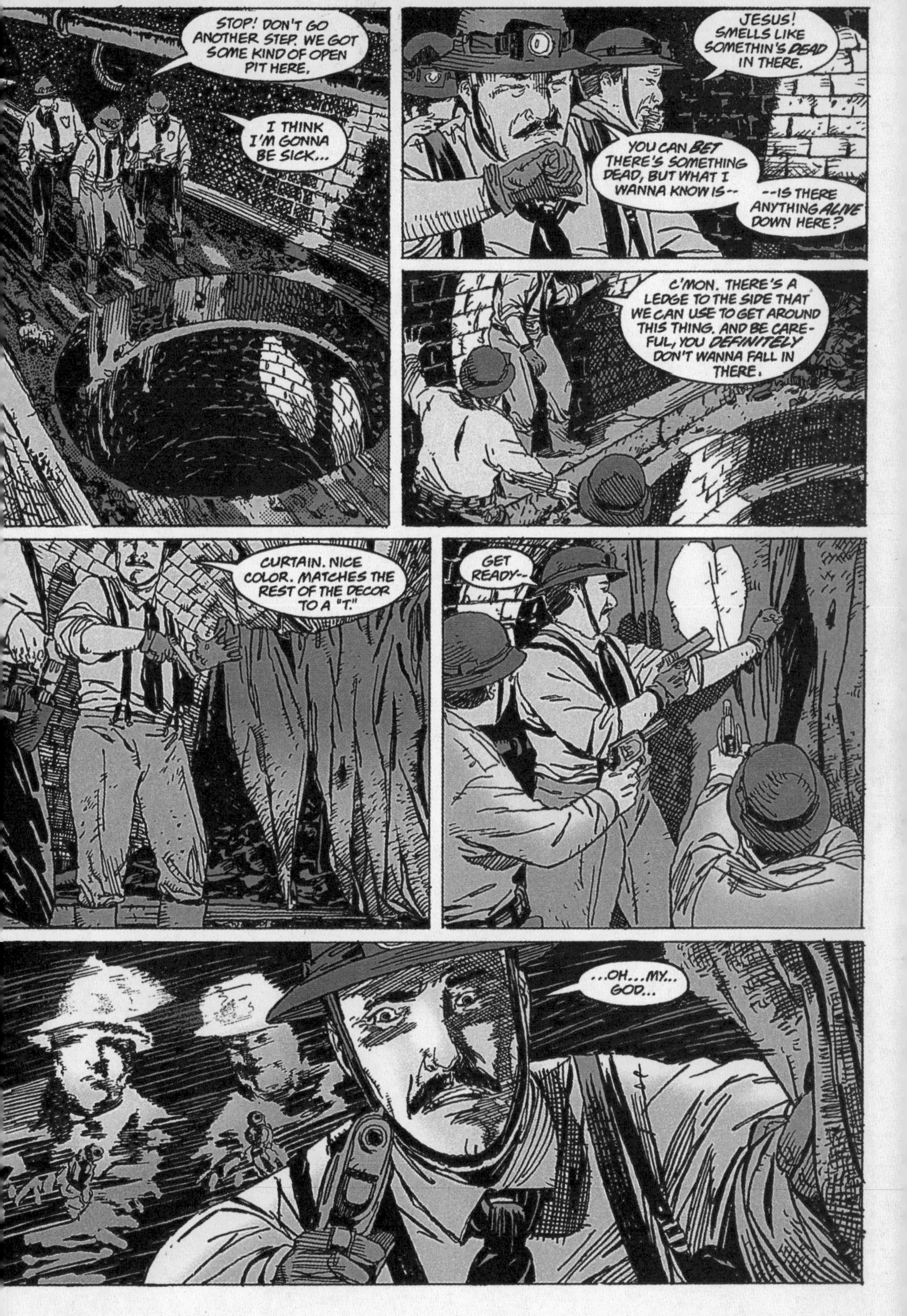
STOP! DON'T GO ANOTHER STEP. WE GOT SOME KIND OF OPEN PIT HERE.
I THINK I'M GONNA BE SICK...
JESUS! SMELLS LIKE SOMETHIN'S DEAD IN THERE.
YOU CAN BET THERE'S SOMETHING DEAD, BUT WHAT I WANNA KNOW IS--
--IS THERE ANYTHING ALIVE DOWN HERE?
C'MON. THERE'S A LEDGE TO THE SIDE THAT WE CAN USE TO GET AROUND THIS THING. AND BE CAREFUL, YOU DEFINITELY DON'T WANNA FALL IN THERE.
CURTAIN. NICE COLOR. MATCHES THE REST OF THE DECOR TO A "T."
GET READY--
...OH...MY... GOD...

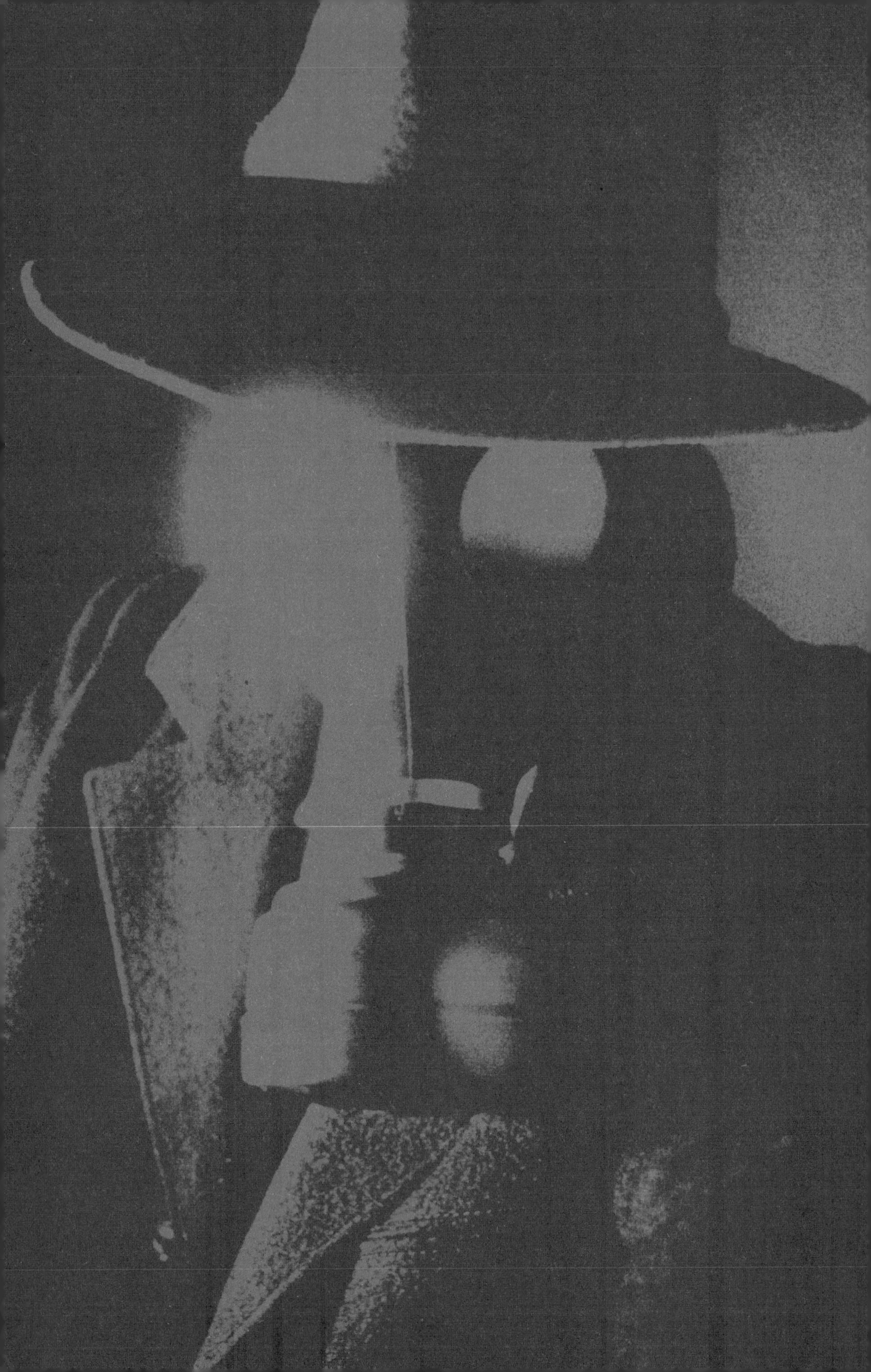

"WE DO NOT SUCCEED..."

WOULD YOU LOOK AT *THAT,* JOE? THEY'RE CLOSED.

IF THAT DOESN'T BEAT *ALL.* WELL, CLAIRE, THERE'S ALWAYS BROCK'S ON BROADWAY.

AGAIN? I'D RATHER EAT MY HAT. WE'LL JUST HAVE SOMETHING AT HOME.

SUIT YOURSELF.

CLOSED

"...WE DO NOT SUCCEED..."

HEY, HENDRICKS? YOU THINK WE SHOULD GO DOWN *IN* THERE? YOU KNOW, *CHECK UP* ON 'EM? THEY BEEN GONE A *WHILE* NOW AN' WE AIN'T HEARD *NOTHIN'.*

ALL *I* KNOW, MATLIN, IS THAT I SURE AM TIRED OF THIS *ROOSTING GIG.*

I'M GETTIN' KINDA *LOGY.* THINK I'LL GRAB SOME JOE. YOU WANT SOME?

NAH, THAT'S OKAY. I GOT SOME *READIN'* HERE GUARANTEED TO KEEP *MY* EYES PEELED WIDE.

"WE DO NOT SUCCEED..."

HENDRICKS? YOU SMELL SOMETHIN' *FUNNY?*

WHAT'D YA *DO?* DROP A *BOMB* AN' LEAVE ME TA--

...SMELL IT...? HUH?

UNHH...

DAMN IT ALL. I FEEL PROUST'S WORDS COMING TO ME, BUT LIKE SO MANY THINGS IN MY LIFE AT THE MOMENT--

--I CAN'T GET PROPER BEARING ON THEM. I CAN'T--

--BRING THEM INTO CLEAR FOCUS.

HOLY JESUS FUCKING CHRIST ON THE CROSS...

LIEUTENANT...?

DON'T EVEN THINK FOR A SECOND THAT *I'VE* GOT ANY ANSWERS TO GIVE YA, FRANCIS--

--'CAUSE THERE *AIN'T* NO ANSWERS FOR *THIS* FUCKIN' HORROR SHOW.

BUT LIEUTENANT, THIS...THIS AIN'T *HUMAN*. *NOBODY* COULD--

FOR THE LOVE OF PETE, FRANCIS. YOU'RE A *COP.* GOTTA KEEP A STIFF UPPER... A STIFF... UH--

UH-- HORRRK!

AH, GEEZ, WHY'D YA HAVE TO GO AN' DO *THAT*? NOW I FEEL LIKE *I'M* GONNA--

2

NIGHT OF THE BUTCHER
FINAL · ACT

THESE DIFFICULTIES WITH MY MEMORY SEEM TO HAVE BEGUN WITH THE DREAMS--

--AND BECOME INCREASINGLY MORE PROBLEMATIC IN THE TIME SINCE.

FWWP

IT SEEMS LOGICAL THAT THE TWO ARE SOMEHOW RELATED.

SPLOOSH

AFTER ALL, I AM A LITTLE YOUNG TO BE INHERITING THE "FAMILY CURSE" AT THIS POINT.

I SEEM TO REMEMBER GRANDFATHER DODDS BEING WELL INTO HIS SIXTIES BEFORE EXHIBITING ANY SYMPTOMS.

OF COURSE ONCE HE BEGAN THE SLIDE--

SPLUSSH

--IT WAS NO TIME BEFORE HE MADE A HEADLONG DASH INTO THE DARKNESS OF HIS DELUSIONS.

4

...YOU BOYS GET THE FEELING WE STUMBLED ONTO THIS CASE A LITTLE LATER THAN WE *SHOULD'VE?*

THIS CHUMP'S EITHER BEEN DEAD FOR *YEARS,* OR...

OR?

OR HE'S BEEN *PICKED* CLEAN.

WHICHEVER WAY IT WENT, THIS IS SOME NASTY WORK.

UH-UH. THIS AIN'T *WORK,* THIS FUCKER'S *HUNTIN'!*

MOST OF *THIS* MEAT'S GONE TO *ROT.*

AND FROM THE *SMELL* OF IT, I'D SAY SOME TIME *BACK,* TO BOOT.

BUT... WHY ARE WE ONLY FINDING OUT ABOUT 'IM *NOW?* WHAT ABOUT ALL THE *FAMILIES* OF THESE PEOPLE?

YOU'D THINK THEY WOULDA FILED MISSING PERSON REPORTS OR--

AH, *YOU* KNOW HOW IT GOES.

PEOPLE UP AN' LEFT THE CITY LOOKIN' FOR SOMETHIN' BETTER WITHOUT SO MUCH AS A "*KISS MY ASS,*" DURIN' THE DEPRESSION.

THESE ARE PROBABLY JUST--

YOU TWO DONE WITH THE SIDESHOW? OR WERE YOU PLANNIN' ON THROWIN' A GOLDFISH DERBY NEXT?

'CAUSE THOUGH I HATE TO BE THE ONE TO *TELL YA--*

-- THE GUIDED TOUR'S NOT *OVER* YET. THERE'S SOME- THIN' MORE BACK HERE...

5

I FEEL SO...ANXIOUS! I DON'T KNOW WHY I EVEN STAY IN THIS CITY AT ALL. I HAVE HALF A MIND TO PACK UP ALL OF MY BELONGINGS AND--AND--

--AND JUST MOVE...TO PARIS! HAVE YOU EVER FELT THAT WAY, DADDY? LIKE YOU HAVE TO GET AWAY FROM EVERYONE--I MEAN, EVERYTHING?

--THAT'S SUN FRESH BISCUITS! THE FRESHNESS OF HOME-BAKED GOODNESS WITH THE ENERGIZING POWER OF THE SUN ITSELF!

AND NOW WE RETURN FOR MORE OF CHRYSLER'S ORIGINAL AMATEUR HOUR AND THE MAN OF THE HOUR... MAJOR BOWES!

NO THANK YOU, SWEETHEART.

DADDY? DID YOU EVEN HEAR WHAT I SAID?

OF COURSE I DID, DIAN, YOU SAID--UH...

WELCOME BACK, VALUED LISTENERS, OUR WEEKLY WHEEL OF FORTUNE GOES A-SPINNING NOW AND WHERE IT STOPS--

OH, NEVER MIND. I'M GOING OUT. AND I'M TAKING THE CAR. DON'T WAIT UP.

THAT'S FINE, DEAR.

FIRST UP TONIGHT, IS AN ENDEARING NEW YOUNG CROONER, TEN-YEAR-OLD ERNEST EMRICOVIK.

ERNEST'S FATHER IS OUT OF WORK, AND YOUNG ERNEST STOLE ALL OF OUR HEARTS WITH HIS DESIRE TO HELP HIS FAMILY THROUGH THE BEAUTIFUL NOISE WE CALL SONG--

OH, AND DADDY? I MAY NOT EVEN COME HOME. I MET THE MOST CHARMING BAND OF GYPSY MEN, AND...WELL, YOU NEVER KNOW.

THAT'S NICE, DIAN.

DIAN...?

SLAM!

--SO LET'S HEAR A BIT OF THAT BEAUTIFUL NOISE NOW--

6

IF THIS DOESN'T BITE MY ASS I SURE AS HELL DON'T KNOW WHAT *WOULD.*

YOU--YOU THINK THIS IS WHERE THE KILLER *LIVES?*

IT AIN'T THE SITE OF THE WORLD'S FAIR, PEA BRAIN.

SPREAD OUT, YOU TWO. TAKE A LOOK AROUND HERE FOR ANYTHING THAT COULD GIVE US THE IDENTITY OF THIS--

HEY, *HERE'S* SOMETHING--

PHOTO, HUH? LOOKS LIKE THE BUTCHER'S GOT SOME FAMILY. *CLOSE* FAMILY.

A LITTLE *TOO* CLOSE FROM THE LOOKS OF THINGS.

LIEUTENANT, GOT A SLEEPING AREA OVER HERE. BLANKETS, PILLOWS...DEFINITELY LOOKS LIVED IN, AND RECENTLY. PRETTY RATTY.

I DON'T THINK YOU'RE GIVIN' RATS ENOUGH *CREDIT.* EVEN *THEY* WOULDN'T LIVE IN *THIS--*

--WHAT HAVE WE *HERE?* WELL, I'LL BE DAMNED...

THESE TWO OZARKS COULD PASS FOR BROTHER AND SISTER.

LOOKS LIKE JUNIOR'S DAD WAS A *VET.* THIS HERE'S A W.W. I MEDAL--

--IN SOME KIND OF *IVORY* BOWL.

HEY...THIS AIN'T A *BOWL...*IT'S A *SKULL!* FUCK!

ALL RIGHT, THAT'S *IT.* WE GOT ENOUGH HERE TO *FRY* THIS BASTARD, BUT WE STILL GOTTA *FIND* HIM.

KELLY, GET BACK OUT TO THE CAR AND RADIO IN FOR SOME SERIOUS BACKUP.

ALONE, SIR?

YES, ALONE! I WANT MORE *MEN,* I WANT *DOGS,* I WANT A FRIGGIN'*CAVALRY UNIT* IN HERE.

FRANCIS, YOU AND ME'LL START CHECKING THE PREMISES.

7

...SURE... SEND *ME* BACK ALONE...

...NO PROBLEM *HERE*, LIEUTENANT ...NO SIREEE...

...'COURSE... DOES GET ME OUTTA THAT DAMNED GHOUL DEN--

CHOK

NNHH! WHA--? WHA--?

NNNN...

NAAAAAAGH!!

WHUKK

...OMIGOD... UHHH... PLEASE... NO--

SHINNNG

SCHWOKK

8

CHOK

IT MUST BE A FRIGHTFUL THING TO SUDDENLY LOSE ONE'S MENTAL ACUITY.

THERE WERE FEW TESTS AVAILABLE FOR GRANDFATHER--

--AND EVEN FEWER TREATMENTS.

THERE WAS NOTHING THE DOCTORS COULD DO TO MAKE HIM WELL AGAIN--

--TO RECONSTRUCT THE PIECES OF THE MAN I KNEW AS AN ILLICIT SUPPLIER OF CLARK'S CARAMELS BEHIND MY FATHER'S BACK.

WHEN HIS DECLINE BEGAN, THOUGH, I WAS TOO YOUNG TO APPRECIATE ITS SEVERITY.

I LAUGHED AT THE GIBBERISH THAT CAME FROM HIS MOUTH AS THOUGH IT WERE SOME ODD BURLESQUE.

-- I FOUND THEM ALL OUTRAGEOUSLY FUNNY, ONLY CORRECTING MY VIEW YEARS LATER--

--WHEN MY FATHER FIRST EXHIBITED SIMILAR SIGNS.

KNOWING THAT AT SOME POINT IN THE FUTURE HE TOO WOULD METAMORPHOSE FROM A MAN I KNEW ALL TOO WELL--

9

--TO A MAN WHO COULD NO LONGER RECOGNIZE THE FACE OF HIS OWN SON.

183

LIEUTENANT? DID YOU *HEAR* SOME-THIN'?

DON'T GO GETTIN' WORKED UP ON ME, FRANCIS. THIS IS A *SEWER.* THERE'S BOUND TA BE *NOISES.*

SOON AS ONE OF 'EM SAYS, "HEY, I'M GONNA *KILL YOU,"* THEN YOU CAN WORRY.

CHRIST! LOOK AT THIS *HAND.*

HMM...NOWHERE NEAR AS FRESH AS ALL THAT OTHER STUFF. HOW LONG HAS THIS NUT BEEN IN BUSINESS?

GEEZ, I HOPE KELLY GETS HERE WITH THAT BACKUP SOON. I'M STARTIN' TO FREEZE TO DEATH.

QUIT *COMPLAININ',* FRANCIS AND CAST A GLANCE *THIS* WAY. WE'VE GOT US SOME SEWING NEEDLES THAT LOOK TO BE MADE FROM BONES. *FINGER BONES,* I'D GUESS.

BONE NEEDLES? WHAT WOULD A GUY NEED BONE NEEDLES FOR?

YOUR AVERAGE JOE *WOULDN'T.* BUT IN CASE IT HASN'T *DAWNED* ON YOU YET, YOUR AVERAGE JOE ALSO WOULDN'T HACK UP PEOPLE'S BODIES AND STORE 'EM IN THE *SEWER* EITHER.

HM. THESE TOOLS LOOK T'BE GOOD AND SHARP.

OUR KILLER MAY BE PRIMITIVE IN *SOME* WAYS, BUT HE'S GOT A FRIGGIN' *DEGREE* IN KNIFE EDGING.

I SURE WISH KELLY'D--

SHIT!

WHAT?

I DIDN'T NOTICE AT FIRST, BUT SOME OF THESE TOOLS ARE *MISSING!*

THAT MEANS HE'S PROBABLY OUT HUNTING RIGHT NOW! WE GOTTA GO FIND KELLY!

10

THE DISEASE, WHATEVER IT WAS, NEVER GOT ITS' CHANCE TO FULLY CLAIM MY FATHER.

IN SOME WAYS I THINK A PRE-EMPTIVE DEATH WAS A FAR BETTER FATE FOR HIM.

HUNHH!

WHONH

MMMAAA!

SMAK

SHWANCK

UNNHH

BETTER TO BE SNATCHED FROM THIS LIFE SCREAMING AND FIGHTING--

UNHH

--THAN TO TRAIL AWAY, A STREAM OF YOUR FORMER SELF.

11

GNNUHAA!

FAR BETTER TO LOOK DEATH SQUARE IN THE EYE--

AAAHNG--

...MY... GOD...

SPLSH

--AND PROCLAIM: "NO. I'LL NAME THE TIME OF OUR MEETING--"

PFFFT

"--IF NOT THE TERMS."

SSST

SSST

DEATH BEING A SINUOUS INTOXI- CATING WOMAN.

NAAAAAH!

FOOOOSSH

AHUK HUK HOFF

HE SAID SHE WOULD COME TO HIM ALL IN PETTICOATS AND CURLS, A BLACK VELVET BODICE--

...NNHNH:

SPASH

--AND WITH THE DARKEST EYES A MAN HAS EVER SEEN, HE SAID SHE LOOKED RIGHT THROUGH HIM.

12

WHEN HE FINALLY SUCCUMBED, I HOPED THAT HE HAD BEEN LUCID--

--THAT HIS FINAL...MOMENTS WERE SPENT ENWRAPPED IN THE ARMS OF A SECRET LOVER--

--RATHER THAN IN THE COLD EMBRACE OF MADNESS.

BUT NONE OF THIS MOVES ME ANY CLOSER TO REMEMBERING PROUST'S STATEMENT BEYOND THE OPENING QUARTET--

"WE DO NOT SUCCEED--"

KELLY? THAT YOU? WHAT THE HELL'S GOIN' ON UP THERE? AND WHAT'S THAT SMELL--?

IDENTIFY YOURSELF, MISTER! NOW!

BLAM

YOU KEEP THAT LIGHT FACIN' ME, OR THE NEXT SHOT GOES THROUGH YOU!

I MEAN IT, BUB! YOU ≈COUGH≈ WAITTAMINUTE ≈COUGH≈ I KNOW THAT SMELL--

SHOOT HIM!

CAN'T! WE DON'T KNOW WHERE ≈COUGH≈ KELLY IS! DAMN IT! TRYIN' TO GET AROUND THIS PIT'S BAD ENOUGH WITHOUT A FUCKIN' GAS CLOUD!

LIEUTENANT! LOOK! DOWN ON THE GROUND--

13

--TELL ME THAT'S NOT KELLY.

OKAY, THAT'S *NOT* KELLY.

NOT UNLESS HE GAINED A FEW HUNDRED POUNDS AND RAN HIS FACE THROUGH A MEAT GRINDER SINCE WE LAST SAW 'IM.

NAH, I'D SAY WE'RE LOOKIN' AT THE FACE OF OUR BUTCHER MAN.

YOU MEAN THE SANDMAN *CAUGHT* HIM? HE HELPED US OUT?

NO HE DIDN'T FUCKING *HELP* US! THAT BASTARD IS A GRADE *A* MENACE, AND NOTHING *BUT*.

MROARR!

OMIGOD! HE'S ALIV-- !EEEAAH!

SSHTHUNK

FRANCIS!

NHH-- HEL--NNAH!

FRANCIS! I CAN'T GET A CLEAR SHOT! FUCK!

DROP HIM, YOU MONSTER, OR I'LL TAKE YOUR UGLY HEAD CLEAN OFF!

UNNAAAN!

OH, GOD, MY CHEST-- HNK--UKK--

14

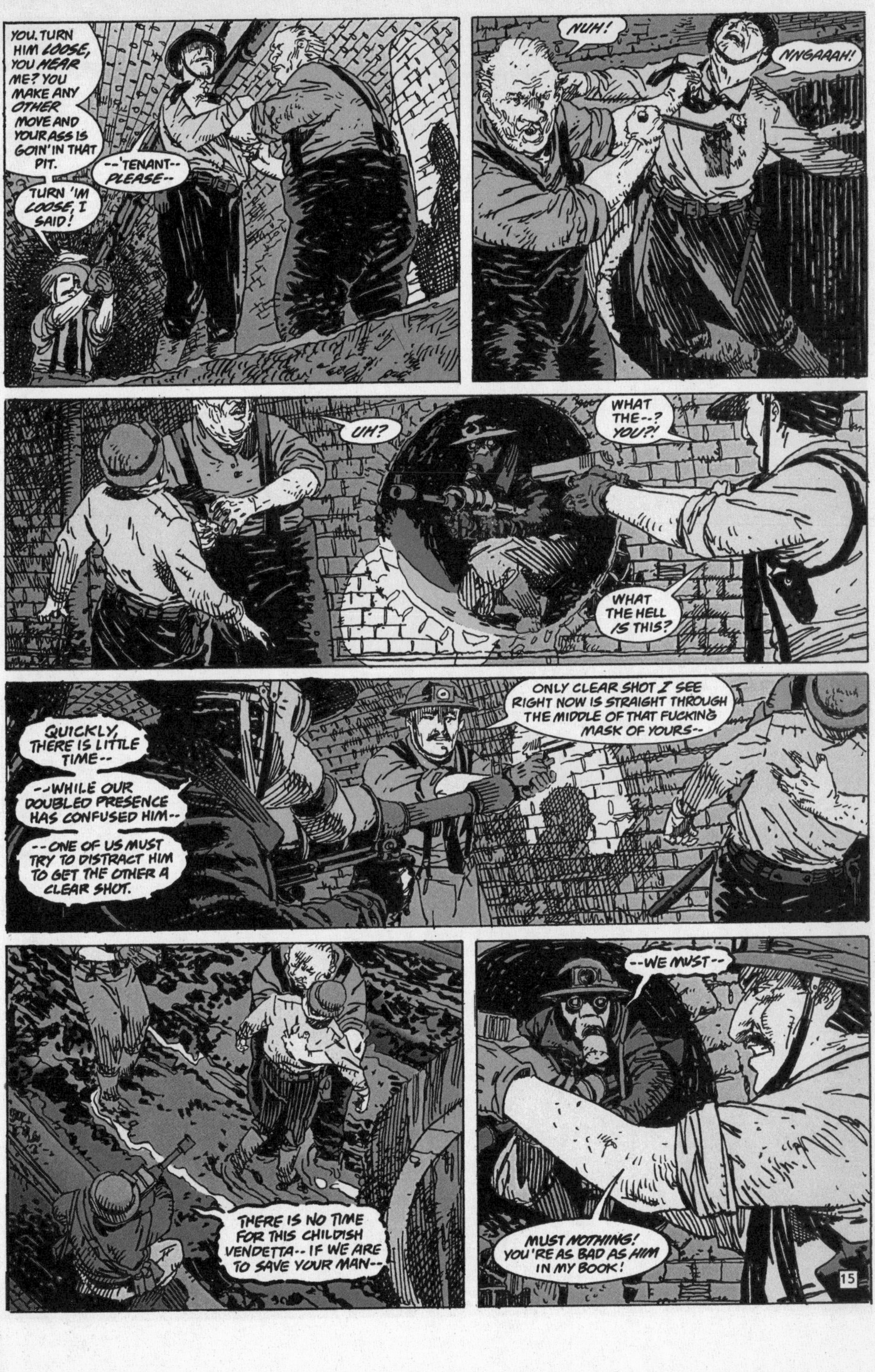
YOU. TURN HIM LOOSE, YOU HEAR ME? YOU MAKE ANY OTHER MOVE AND YOUR ASS IS GOIN' IN THAT PIT.
--'TENANT-- PLEASE--
TURN 'IM LOOSE, I SAID!
NUH!
NNGAAAH!
UH?
WHAT THE--? YOU?!
WHAT THE HELL IS THIS?
QUICKLY, THERE IS LITTLE TIME--
--WHILE OUR DOUBLED PRESENCE HAS CONFUSED HIM--
--ONE OF US MUST TRY TO DISTRACT HIM TO GET THE OTHER A CLEAR SHOT.
ONLY CLEAR SHOT I SEE RIGHT NOW IS STRAIGHT THROUGH THE MIDDLE OF THAT FUCKING MASK OF YOURS--
THERE IS NO TIME FOR THIS CHILDISH VENDETTA--IF WE ARE TO SAVE YOUR MAN--
--WE MUST--
MUST NOTHING! YOU'RE AS BAD AS HIM IN MY BOOK!
15

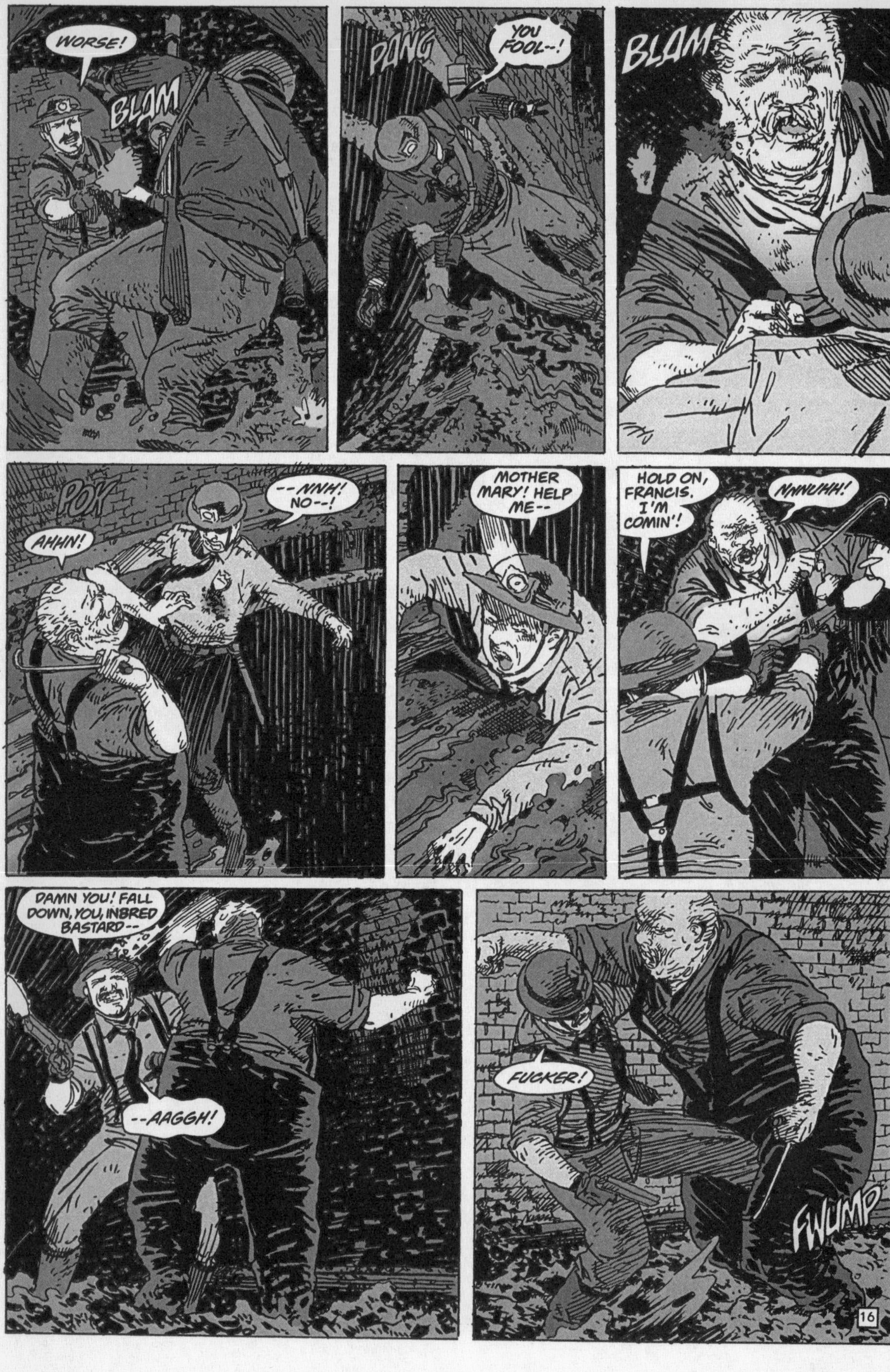
WORSE!
BLAM
PANG
YOU FOOL--!
BLAM
POK
--NNH! NO--!
AHHN!
MOTHER MARY! HELP ME--
HOLD ON, FRANCIS. I'M COMIN'!
NNNUHH!
BLAM
DAMN YOU! FALL DOWN, YOU, INBRED BASTARD--
--AAGGH!
FUCKER!
FWUMP
16

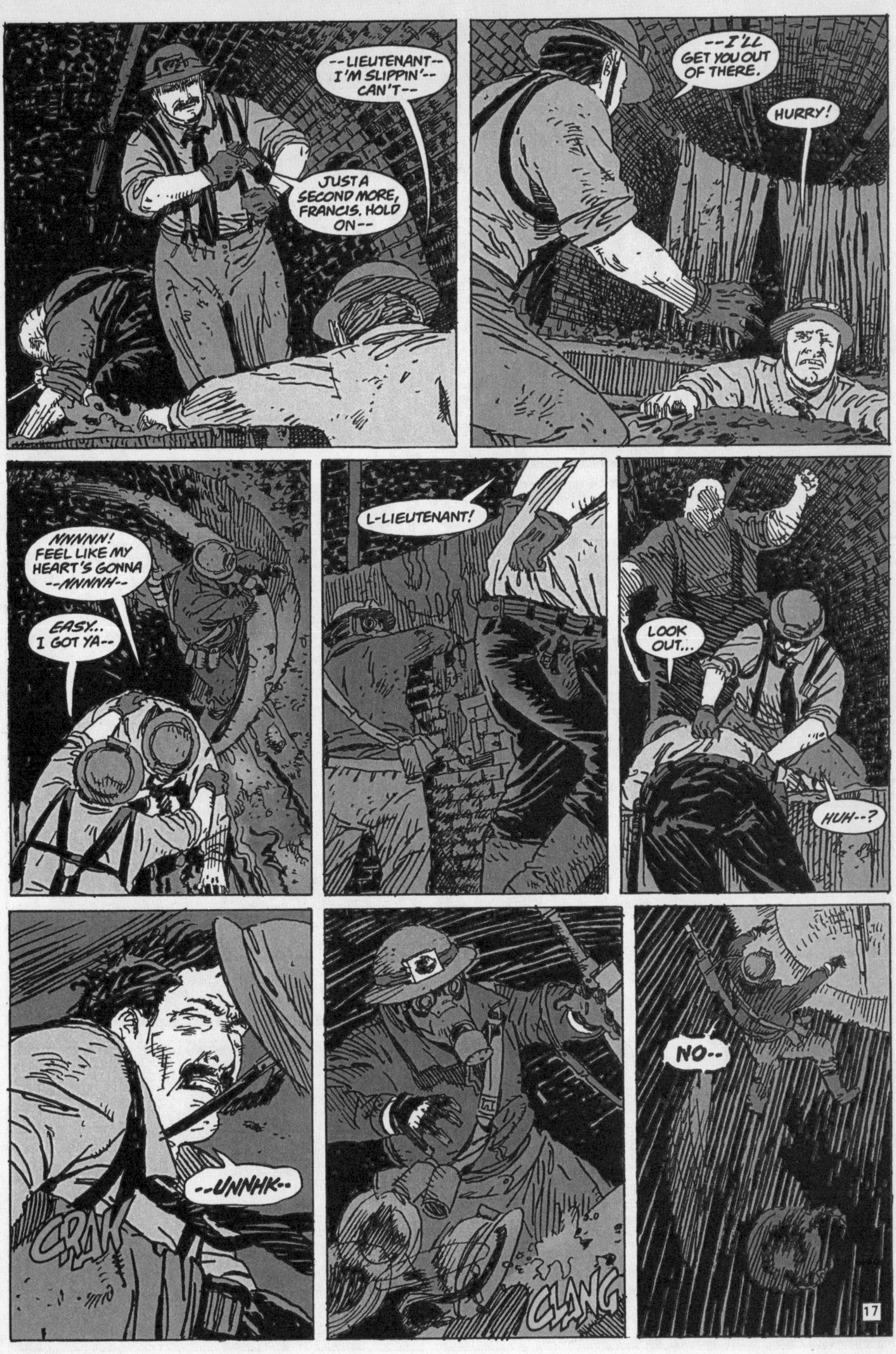
--LIEUTENANT--
I'M SLIPPIN'--
CAN'T--
JUST A SECOND MORE, FRANCIS. HOLD ON--
--I'LL GET YOU OUT OF THERE.
HURRY!
NNNNN! FEEL LIKE MY HEART'S GONNA --NNNNH--
EASY... I GOT YA--
L-LIEUTENANT!
LOOK OUT...
HUH--?
--UNNHK--
CRAK
CLANG
NO--
17

I OFTEN WONDER WHAT MY FATHER'S LIFE MIGHT HAVE BEEN LIKE IF HE HADN'T PASSED WHEN HE DID.

UNNNHH

TOK

WOULD I HAVE BEEN ABLE TO WATCH HIM SUFFER THROUGH THE LOSS OF HIS LIFE LONG BEFORE ITS ACTUAL CONCLUSION? THE WAY HE HAD WATCHED HIS FATHER BEFORE HIM?

I LIKE TO THINK HE WOULD HAVE FOUGHT THE CURSE.

DANGER

DANGER

CLANK

THAT HE WOULD HAVE REELED BACK IN EVERYTHING HE LOST AND PUT A STOP TO IT RIGHT THERE.

TOK
TOK

IT'S A BELIEF THAT I PROBABLY CARRY AS MUCH FOR MYSELF AS FOR HIM--

18

-- BUT I LIKE TO THINK HE WOULD HAVE SUCCEEDED.

"WE DO NOT SUCCEED..."

THE WORDS COME BACK TO ME.

AND YET... I'M NO LONGER INTIMIDATED BY THEIR LACK OF RESOLUTION.

OOOHHHH...

INSTEAD I TAKE THE OPENING AS A CHALLENGE.

...MUHTHUHHH...

THE WORDS I NEED ARE OUT THERE--

...HURRD MUHTHUHH...

HURRD! NNH!

...MH... HURRD...

--IF I CAN ONLY WILL MYSELF TO HEAR THEM.

19

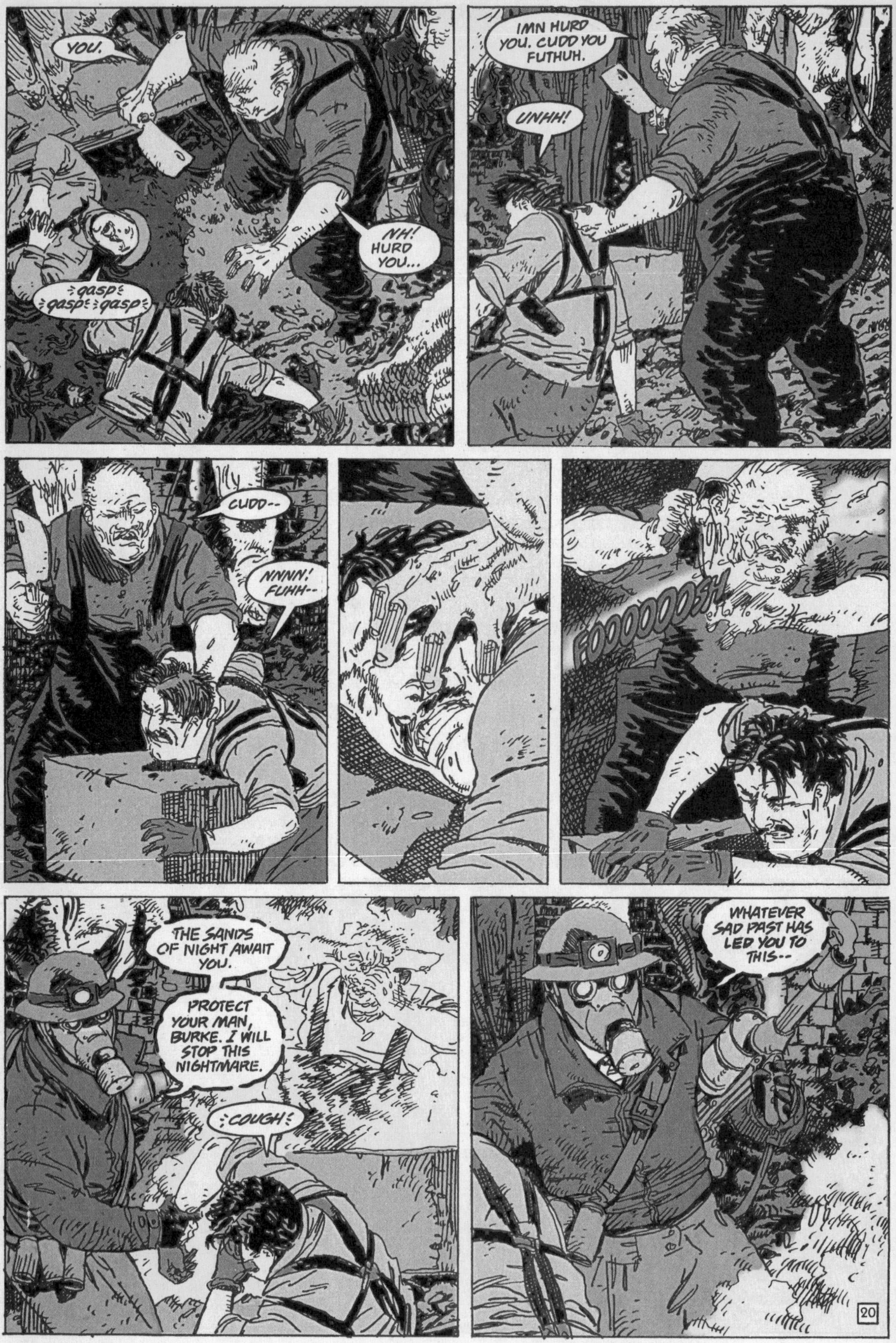
YOU.
NH! HURD YOU...
gasp gasp gasp
IMN HURD YOU. CUDD YOU FUTHUH.
UNHH!
CUDD--
NNNN! FUHH--
FOOOOOOSH
THE SANDS OF NIGHT AWAIT YOU.
PROTECT YOUR MAN, BURKE. I WILL STOP THIS NIGHTMARE.
COUGH!
WHATEVER SAD PAST HAS LED YOU TO THIS--
20

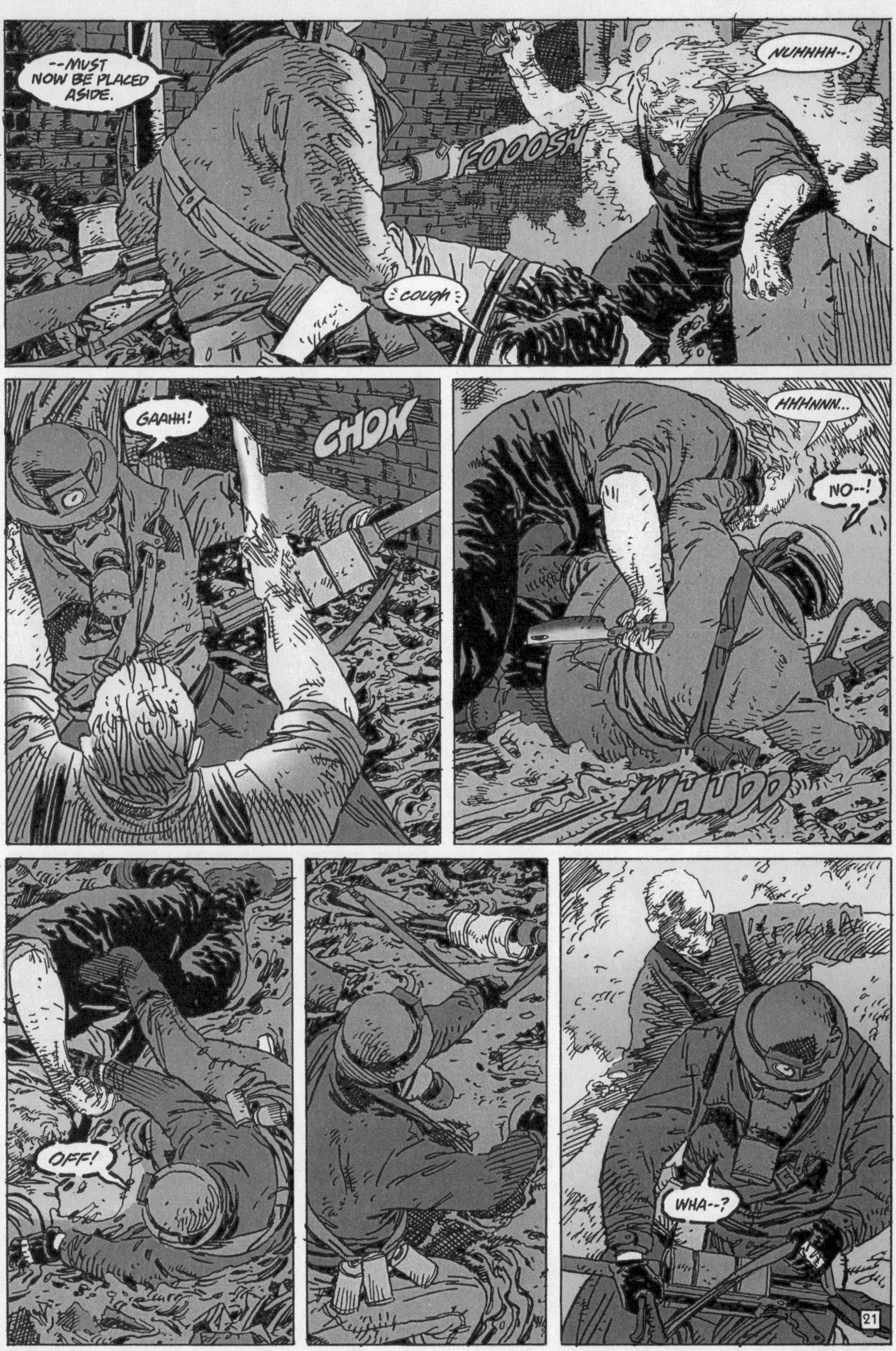
--MUST NOW BE PLACED ASIDE.
NUHHHH--!
FOOOSH
cough
GAAHH!
CHON
HHHNNN...
NO--!
WHUDD
OFF!
WHA--?
21

SUDDENLY PROUST'S WORDS COME RACING BACK TO ME--

NUHHHH--!

--CLEAR, COMPLETE, CONCISE.

BROM

THUD!

ONE DOWN, ;COUGH; ONE TO--TO--

;COUGH;
--TO GO--
OOOH...
SHIT...
GASSED
AGAII--

MY ELUSIVE MEMORY RETURNS WITH A SIMPLICITY, A SENSE OF RIGHTNESS I'D FEARED HAD LEFT ME FOREVER.

LIEUTENANT?

NO, NOT OVER THERE, THIS WAY.

YEAH, SHOT CAME FROM UP AHEAD THERE.

"WE DO NOT SUCCEED--"

22

"--IN CHANGING THINGS ACCORDING TO OUR--"

"--DESIRE--"

"--BUT GRADUALLY--"

"--OUR DESIRE CHANGES."

SCREEECH

--EH?

GOIN' MY WAY, STRANGER?

CLICK

DIAN?

I'M GOING ANY WAY THE POLICE AREN'T AT THE MOMENT.

TO SAY I'M GLAD TO SEE YOU... WOULD BE AN UNDERSTATEMENT.

MY DESIRES HAVE CHANGED.

I SENSE OTHER CHANGES AWAIT ME AS WELL.

I EXPECT THAT MANY MORE RESTLESS NIGHTS LIE AHEAD--

--BUT I NOW FEEL THAT I WON'T BE FACING THEM ALONE.

THE·END

DC
VERTIGO
MATT WAGNER
STEVEN T. SEAGLE
SANDMAN MYSTERY THEATRE
GUY DAVIS
VINCE LOCKE
NO. 21
DEC 94
$1.95 US
$2.75 CAN
£1.25 UK
SUGGESTED FOR MATURE READERS
"...DEEP IN THE UNYIELDING SHADOWS, HIS FATAL DIAGNOSIS WAS CAST IN INK."
ACT 1 dr. death OF 4
GAVIN WILSON
RICHARD BRUNING

DC
VERTIGO
.22
.N 95
95 US
.75 CAN
.25 UK
SUGGESTED
FOR MATURE
READERS
MATT WAGNER
STEVEN T. SEAGLE
GUY DAVIS
VINCE LOCKE
SANDMAN MYSTERY THEATRE
"...THE SONATA CUT SHORT BY AN UNEXPECTED NOTE."
ACT 2 dr. death OF 4
GAVIN WILSON
RICHARD BRUNING

DC
VERTIGO
NO. 23
FEB 95
$1.95 US
$2.75 CAN
£1.25 UK
SUGGESTED FOR MATURE READERS
MATT WAGNER
STEVEN T. SEAGLE
GUY DAVIS
VINCE LOCKE
SANDMAN MYSTERY THEATRE
"...SKIN ON SKIN, THEIR SECRETS FELL AWAY WITH THE NIGHT."
ACT 3 dr.death OF 4
GAVIN WILSON
RICHARD BRUNING

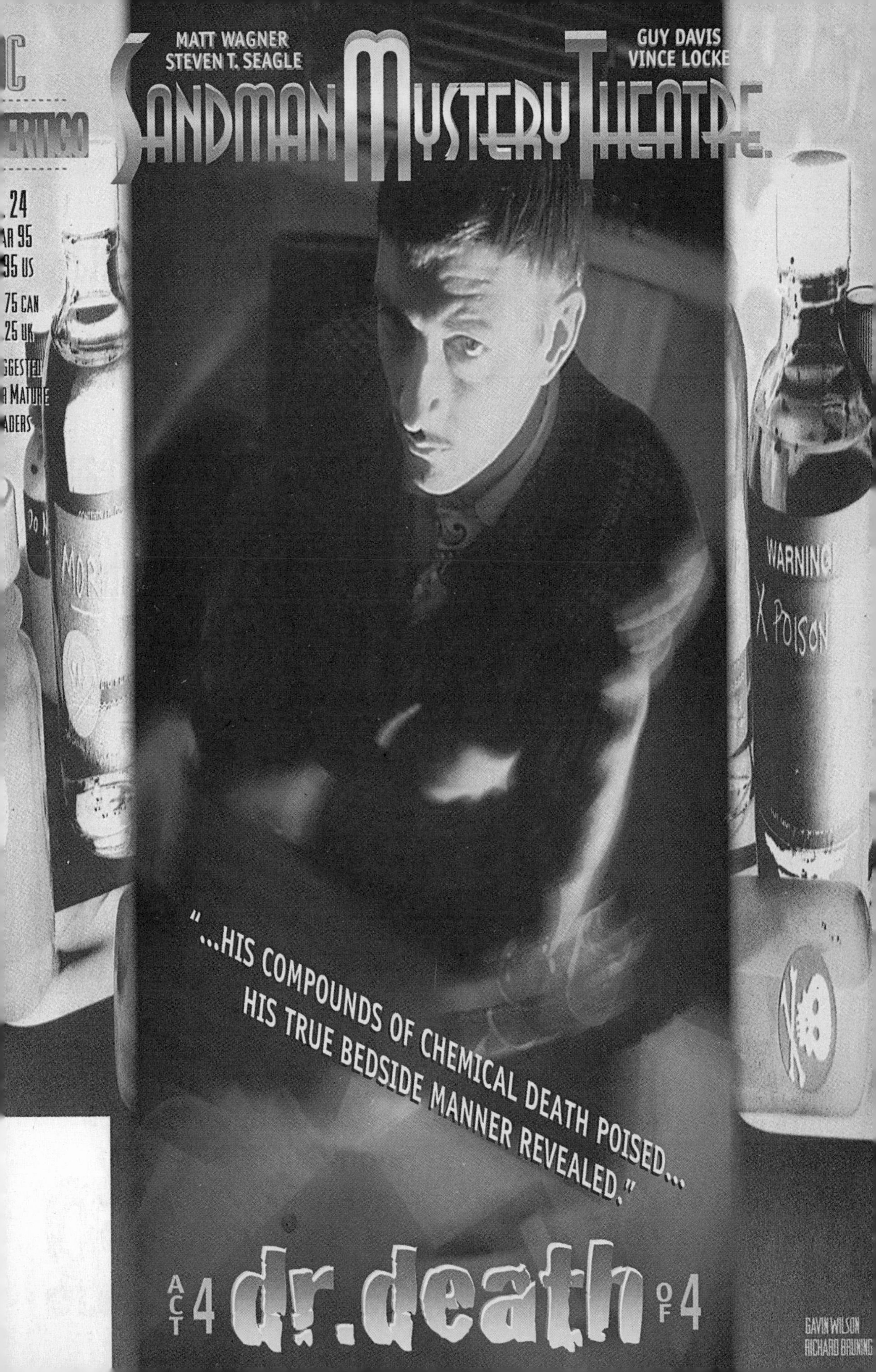
MATT WAGNER
STEVEN T. SEAGLE
GUY DAVIS
VINCE LOCKE
SANDMAN MYSTERY THEATRE
. 24
AR 95
95 US
75 CAN
25 UK
GGESTED
R MATURE
ADERS
WARNING
X POISON
"...HIS COMPOUNDS OF CHEMICAL DEATH POISED...
HIS TRUE BEDSIDE MANNER REVEALED."
ACT 4 dr.death OF 4
GAVIN WILSON
RICHARD BRUNING

matt wagner · steven t. seagle · guy davis

SANDMAN MYSTERY THEATRE

DC

VERTIGO

NO. 25
APR 95
$1.95 US
$2.75 CAN
£1.25 UK

SUGGESTED
FOR MATURE
READERS

"...the clang of metal, the rush of blood and the stench of broken dreams."

NIGHT OF THE BUTCHER
ACT 1 OF 4

GAVIN WILSON · RICHARD BRUNING

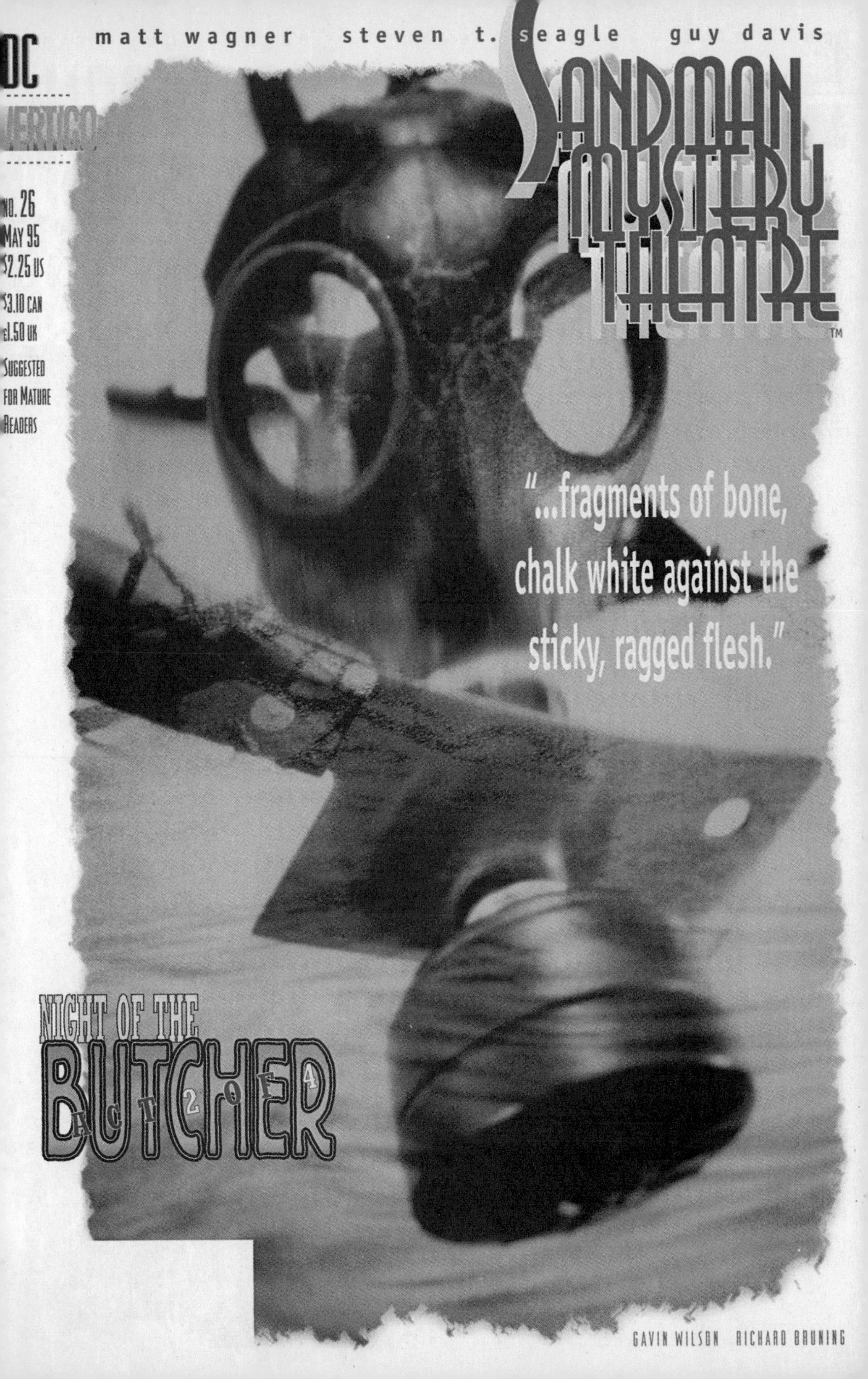

DC
VERTIGO
matt wagner steven t. seagle guy davis
SANDMAN MYSTERY THEATRE
TM
NO. 26
MAY 95
$2.25 US
$3.10 CAN
£1.50 UK
SUGGESTED FOR MATURE READERS
"...fragments of bone, chalk white against the sticky, ragged flesh."
NIGHT OF THE BUTCHER
ACT 2 OF 4
GAVIN WILSON RICHARD BRUNING

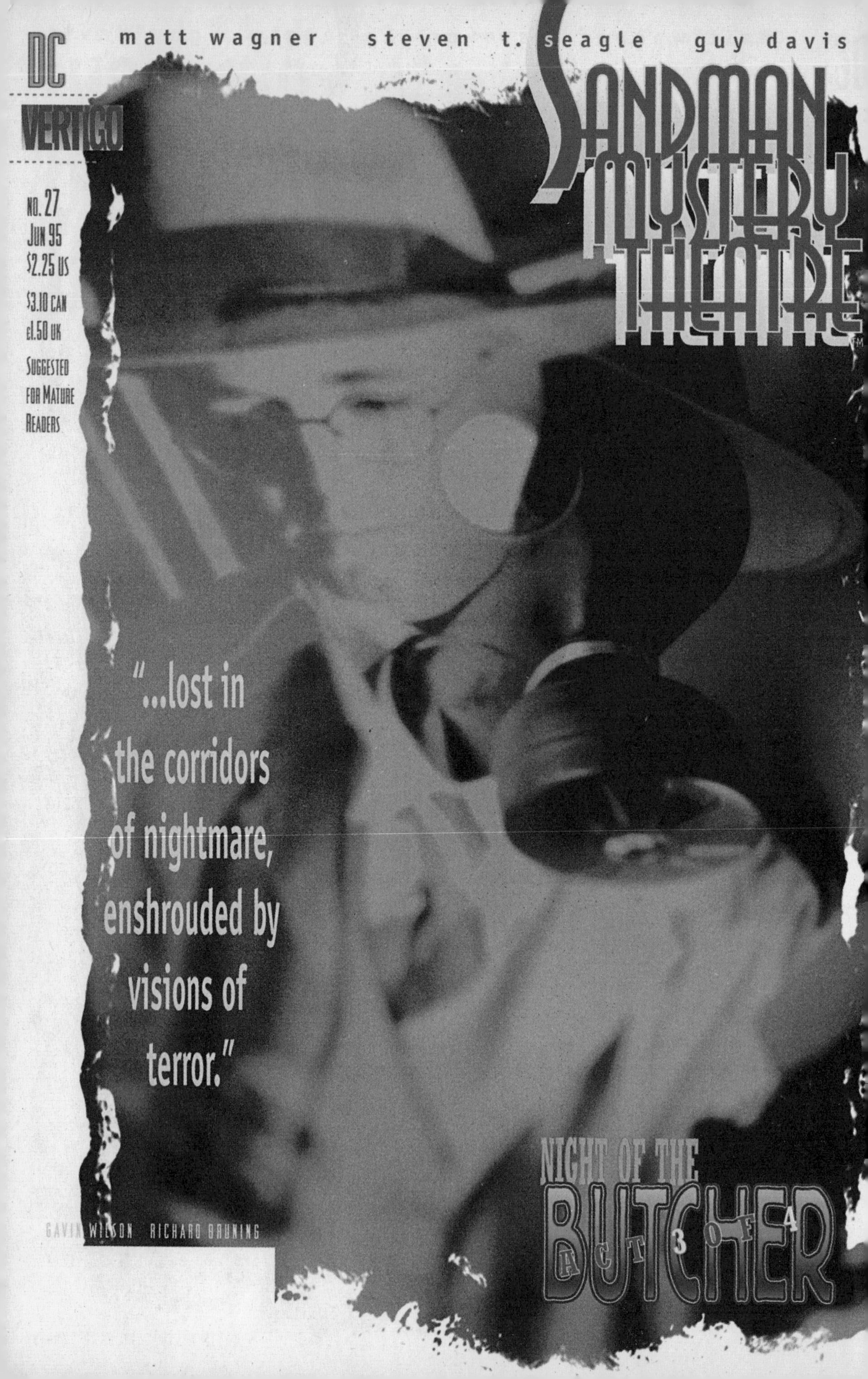
DC
VERTIGO
matt wagner steven t. seagle guy davis
SANDMAN MYSTERY THEATRE
NO. 27
JUN 95
$2.25 US
$3.10 CAN
£1.50 UK
SUGGESTED FOR MATURE READERS
"...lost in the corridors of nightmare, enshrouded by visions of terror."
NIGHT OF THE BUTCHER
ACT 3 OF 4
GAVIN WILSON RICHARD BRUNING